# Gracefully Broken

ISBN : 978-1-965593-15-8
Copyright © 2023 Gracefully Broken
Published by Cornerstone Publishing
Info@thecornerstonepublishers.com
www.thecornerstonepublishers.com

Unless otherwise stated, scripture quotations are taken from KJV and NIV versions of the Bible.

Edited and Published in Kenya in 2023 by The Excellent Man Publishers.

Design, and layout by The Excellent Man publishers.
Cell: +254 732 007 060
Email. davgreatness@gmail.com

# Contents

# Dedication

I dedicate this book to my children Arthur and Hadassah, who started the journey with me from the beginning. My restoration testimony additional gifts; my husband Mr. Frank Atsulu, children;- Anne, Mitchelle (our smiling machine), Emmanuel, Joshua (our other smiling machine) and Chris. Your love and support has seen this come to success.

My parents Mr. & Mrs. Benedict and Lucy Kibe, I would never trade you for anything. You have supported me throughout my seasons and always made me comfortable at home. I love you to the galaxies and back. My brothers Maurice Kibe, Martin Kibe and Michael Kibe, you are the best siblings in the whole world. My sister Winnie Mugo, you filled the big sister gap so well, my confidant and friend, thank you for cheering me on.

My faith parents Bishop Erick Mwangi and Rev Vicky Mwangi, you held my hands when I was emotionally unstable and guided me into purpose. Under your counsel God changed my garments from ashes into beauty, may God reward you for me. Seasons of my life have transitioned for better under your counsel.

More grace to you.

# Acknowledgements

To my heavenly father for His grace through the seasons of life that have made this book. Daddy I am grateful for preservation. You carried me through to the glory and honor of your name. Jehovah I give you all the glory. Your daughter is grateful Yahweh.

To my mother in the faith Rev Vicky Mwangi, for encouraging and urging me to write this book, for being a strong pillar, walking with me in the book writing journey without whom this book would not exist.

To my children who cheered me on even when they didn't understand what mummy was up to, I love you too much.

To Marion Gitau for helping me put my thoughts into words through interviews.

To everyone that I have had an opportunity to interact with throughout this journey.

# Foreword

The journey of finding your purpose is like a puzzle that has to fit on the puzzle board.

The ups and downs all end up as a beautiful result.
Walking the journey of purpose needs the intervention of God to help navigate the seasons.

Gracefully broken is one such a journey that has the fingerprints of God all over it.

The author Susan Kibe has authentically shared her journey to help the reader pick some lessons from it.

This book is a must read for everyone who needs to find direction.
The patterns of life in our background should not be a hindrance to our growth and finding purpose.

Seasons of pain and loss should not define our destiny since that is already planned by God when He created us. Believers are called to a life of accountability to help them navigate life seasons.

The desire of God for His children is to learn from instructions and not experience.

Where life experiences happen however, it is important to pick the lessons from it so as not to waste any season.

Every season we go through in life has lessons for us to pick and learn from.

As her mentor, I have seen her rise up from deep pain and loss of direction to a season of settling.

**Faith Muriithi**
**FAMU Mentorship.**

# 1

## Genesis of Susan Kibe

It was the wee hours of a cold Friday morning on the slopes of Mount Kenya in a simple town called Nyeri. A clerk in his mid 30s working for Ministry of Public Works and his wife, a 30 year old secretary in the Ministry of Cooperative were blessed with a baby girl. This was the first girl, the last born child and it was a happy moment, the joy that filled their hearts for beholding a baby girl was evident on their faces. This girl born after three brothers was a sight to behold as the elder brothers kept checking out their baby sister.

This beautiful girl continued to grow well, in good health as her parents raised her in a home full of warmth and love. When she turned around 3 years, her parents noticed her legs were not developing as expected. Upon some check up and tests she was found to have a deformity that made her to wear special shoes from the Association of Physically Disabled Kenya. That was the first file that would be opened with her name on it out of the ordinary. This girl was none other than Susan Kibe, beloved daughter of Mr Benedict Kibe and Mrs. Lucy Nyambura Kibe.

To the Glory of God, My legs got healed completely and that attack did not triumph. From that tender age I can attest that God was holding my life together for a divine purpose. The hand of God was strongly on me from that tender age.

My education journey started at Ministry of Public Works Nursery School which was a walking distance from home. My father would take me to school as he went to work. I did my two years of Nursery and joined Nyamachaki Primary school where I studied from Standard 1 to 4. In 1992 my parents moved to our current resident where they built a home and so we left the Ministry quarters. That meant I was in a new environment alone since my brothers were in boarding high schools. My parents thought it wise to enroll me into a boarding school so that I can focus on my studies. It was actually fun to join a boarding school then, as most of my friends were in boarding school too.

I joined Tetu Girls Primary Boarding School and repeated class 4 since I was very tiny and a very poor feeder. Joining Boarding school at such a tender age taught me how to be independent, responsible, and I also got exposed to a different way of life. Homesick became a part of life every first week after opening school but it was an amazing experience for me. I actually made great friends who we are in touch even today.

My boarding season gave me great experience all round. First, I was able to be independent at an early age. I would do things on my own like making my bed, washing my clothes and even making sure that I take care of my stuff as my mum was not with me. Raising a child from the early years to be independent has a life-long impact. At a very basic level, independent children are confident, competent and able to take care of themselves in all situations. Being allowed to do things for themselves, they tend to be self-driven and need minimal external validation of their achievements. That became of me.

This category of children, also make good and informed decisions, by being allowed to consider various options from a very young age. They are both trusting and trust-worthy, from knowing the meaning of responsibility and accountability for being allowed to complete tasks on their own. Life skills start in the early years of a child's life, just as they are discovering the world.

However, in as much as I was happy to be in a new environment, I sometimes felt that I was too young to be separated from my parents. This however, didn't deter me from working hard in school.

I progressed well with my studies and was an above average student. I sat my Kenya Certificate of Primary Education and got admission in Chinga Girls High School which was a provincial school, an equivalent of Extra county in the current system. My high school journey was smooth apart from an altitude sickness I developed in Form 2 after hiking Mt. Kenya. I got healed and escaped a bone marrow transplant which had been prescribed because I had become anaemic. That was another phase of my life that God Glorified Himself yet again. My mother walked very closely with me in this season. I completed high school and perfomed below my expectation but managed to join Jomo Kenyatta University of Agriculture and Technology for my BSc- IT. In four years I graduated with second class honors and started internship immediately. God still held me up with His righteous hand.

# Christian Foundation

I grew up in a very religious home, a Christian home. My parents being staunch Catholics instilled in me the fear of God from my early childhood. I learnt from an early age that I am whom I am because of Christ. In our home you either loved church or loved church. There was no option. This was the greatest gift our parents gave us in our tender age. They showed us the house of God and they took us there.

The bible states in
**Proverbs 22:6** *"Train a child in the way he should go, and when he is old he will not turn from it."*

This scripture has really turned out to be true to us.
The Word of God is the most efficient, tried and tested tool for training. This WORD is God-breathed and is useful for teaching, rebuking, correcting and training. Teaching children the truths of Scripture will make them wise for salvation, thoroughly equip them to do good works, prepare them to give an answer to everyone who asks them the reason for their life, and prepare them to withstand the different cultures bent on indoctrinating young people with secular values.

*"Sons are a heritage from the LORD, children a reward from him."*
**Psalms 127:3**
It would certainly seem fitting, then, that we heed the wise counsel to train them appropriately. In fact, the value that God placed on teaching our children the truth is clearly addressed by Moses who stressed to his people the importance of teaching their children about the Lord and His

commands and laws:

### See Deuteronomy 6:7-9
*"Impress them on your children.*
*Talk about them when you sit at home and when you walk along the road,*
*When you lie down and when you get up.*
*Tie them as symbols on your hands and bind them on your foreheads.*
*Write them on the doorframes of your houses and your gates"*

Training up children in the way they should go means, first and foremost, directing them to the ways of God. When I was 11 years, I was taught catechism. This is a summary or exposition of catholic doctrine and serves as a learning introduction to the sacrament.

I attended the catechism class with enthusiasm and I was excited to learn the teachings of the Catholic faith which included the creed, sacraments, commandments, and prayers.

# 2

# My Parents Impact

I had a normal upbringing and I enjoyed the company of my family just like any other child. I didn't have favor by being the last born as I was not accorded any special attention. I was a disciplined child from an early age and this made my parents to love me unconditionally. Discipline is an integral part of raising godly children, because the LORD disciplines those he loves, as a father the son he delights in

**Proverbs 3:12**
*Thus, we should neither take discipline lightly nor become disheartened.*
**See Proverbs 3.7** - *Do not be wise in your own eyes; fear the LORD and shun evil.*
*8 This will bring health to your body and nourishment to your bones.*
*9 Honor the LORD with your wealth, with the firstfruits of all your crops;*
*10 then your barns will be filled to overflowing, and your vats will brim over with new wine.*
*Verse 12 because the LORD disciplines those he loves, as a father the son he delights in.*

Likewise, when we discipline our children, they receive wisdom and they bring us peace and respect. In fact, even at a tender age children are able to discern that discipline is rooted in love. That is why children who grow up in homes without discipline often feel unloved and are more likely to disobey authority as they grow older. Now, the discipline administered to any child should be in accordance to the offense and physical discipline. Indeed, discipline, though it may seem unpleasant when received, will produce a *"harvest of righteousness and peace for those who have been trained by it"*.

Parents should have the same zeal for teaching their children what is right. Parents have been given the privilege of being stewards of their children's lives for a very short time, but the teaching and training they provide will remain with the children even as they grow older. According to the promise of Proverbs, a child who is diligently trained in the *"way he should go"* will remain true to that way in this life and reap its rewards all through.

Back to my life expectations, I always had this picture in mind that I will have a great life ahead of me. I would picture myself having a great family with wonderful children whom I was to give my best in life. I had a picture of a perfect life, and aspired a better life.

I wanted to be a successful lawyer when I grow up as I admired to be called a *"learned person"*. This made me work hard in school. I was glad to have parents who impacted my life positively and who were working hard to build me up, helping me create belief in myself.

One of parental duties my parents did was affirmation, which over the years I've seen the power of us as parents, affirming our children.

When we affirm our children, we need to do so using methods they understand. As parents, we should be Intentional in praise and affirmation. We should also be specific by using our words to empower our children towards achieving greater success in their day-to-day accomplishments. As an only girl in the family, my mom and dad told me I could do anything in the world. This should not be generic, but purposeful and directed. And when you have more than one child, it is crucial to ensure that you affirm all your children. We may not be saying the same words for each child (because each one of them is different), but we can choose to affirm each of them commenting on a particular strength or on a specific positive behavior. Phrases like, *"you are a good swimmer"*, *"you are a good driver"*. *"You will excel in your school work"*, goes a long way in motivating our children. Affirmation helps to shape the destiny of the children. Girls need to be told they are beautiful by their dads. Doting on them makes sure that no joker will succeed to lure them with words. They will have already heard it from daddy and so will be confident to make sound decisions. The first date a girl should have is with her father; it sets the standard for her future engagements with men.

### So how do we really affirm our children?
With a deep acceptance and appreciation of the developing person he or she is; and not for the behavior that he or she exhibits.

In my case, my mom used to tell me that I could be the best and that I could accomplish anything. She always gave me a high level of belief in myself. My siblings echoed the same kind of motivational support. For our identity and personhood is largely nurtured from as far back as we can remember; and as young children, it is our parents who help shape the foundations of what we feel about ourselves and how we deal with who we are as a person. While growing up, I was surrounded not by wealth, but by upbeat, positive, possibility thinking people. Home is where we learn and understand who we are, school teaches what we can be, but the **"WHO AM I"** question is answered at home.

Surround yourself with people who build you up. The power of association and disassociation is a very important power for you to exercise in your life. Get away from people who pull you down and get around people who give you belief. Even though I never furthered my education in law studies but rather chose a different path, I excelled well in my high school studies and later became an IT specialist; I was content that I achieved great success in my education. I graduated in 2006 from JKUAT with BSc IT (Second upper)

Though it feels great to chase our goals, it is very important to be content with what God has given us rather than chasing everything that we think is better for us. These days, we need everything in the world, even the things we don't really need; because we saw them with someone else, and it looks fit or right for the person, out of greed, we feel it will be right for us. Our assumptions make us yearn for what we have no ability of, and what we have no capacity to either contain or retain.

Being content is massively advantageous in many ways. To some, they don't think it is, but in my strong opinion, it is everything that life needs. Lack of contentment puts people in a state of desperation, and a desperate person can do anything, especially negative things. Count yourself lucky if you escape the mayhem of a desperate person. Some of the advantages of being content are that it creates;

**Peace:** the peace of being you is not comparable to anything. The peace of not caring what anyone thinks, but simply going ahead to live your own life is unimaginable. Some people kill themselves over what other people think. People don't realize how important inner peace is until they lose it and when they lose it, their whole world falls apart. Contentment comes with moderate living; not living beyond your means, not buying beyond what you can afford, and even if you can afford it, you consider the poor and decide not to be extravagant when there are people that can't afford one square meal in a day. The highly spiritual beings that have gone through this world were very contented people, and for that, they were able to live exemplary lives and left enduring legacies worth emulating behind. We read of people like Mahatma Gandhi, and more, who were very content people, and today, we all make references to their legacies because of the sacrifices they made.

**Indebtedness:** One huge gain in being content is you never borrow to fund a lifestyle. Some people spend over one year repaying the loans they took to host a wedding ceremony. The question is 'were they under compulsion to host an expensive wedding?' The answer is no! They probably did it because a friend did the same. The friend they copied won't help them repay the loans. The friend may not even know they took a loan to impress other people for a few hours. It is unwise to take a loan to finance avoidable budgets all because of not being content with what you can afford.

**Competition:** contentment takes you out of the circle of unnecessary and unhealthy competition. Some people want to outdo everybody even if they don't have the means to do it. My take is even if you do have the means; you don't need to be in competition with people because you want to prove that you're better. There are far better places to score points rather than grounds of no real values. If you borrow to compete for things of no profitable outcomes, you will eventually have difficulties repaying. Don't buy a hundred-thousand-dollar car when you live in a one-dollar house. Which one enhances in value; the car or the house? Your car will depreciate in value while your house will appreciate.

*Focus*: a content person is far more focused than the one not contented. Because he isn't in unhealthy competition with anyone, or trying to outdo his neighbors, all his concentrations are on his dreams or goals. With high concentrations, he gets his goals achieved on time. Those who worry over what people think about what they eat, drink, or wear, hardly achieve anything credibly substantial. Always wishing you were married to your friend's wife stopped you from developing your wife, children and home as a whole. The beauty in the other woman is hidden in your wife, but your lack of focus has prevented you from bringing it out of her. If only you focus on how to build your very own, you will be inundated with so much you have but never knew you had because you weren't content with what you had.

*Good health:* some people are insomniac because they spend sleepless nights thinking where they will get the money to fund an unnecessarily ostentatious adventure. Some people develop high blood pressure worrying how their children will become doctors even if they can't solve physics calculations or balance a chemical equation, all because their neighbor's son just gained admission into medical school. Rather than focus on the uniqueness of their children, they look outside the window and die over another person's nature. Contentment gives you peace of mind, and peace of mind gives you good health.

***Your own Pace:*** everyone has his pace, and for the fact they can't move at another person's pace does not mean they can't be champions in their own categories. Usain Bolt is a sprinter. Eliud Kipchoge is a marathoner. If you tell Bolt to compete against Kipchoge in a marathon, he will be considered a failure. If you tell both of them to compete in sprint, Kipchoge will be a failure. Many people have been judged failures because they competed in events that have nothing to do with their nature, uniqueness and commitment. Contentment makes you run at your own pace. It makes you follow your nature, uniqueness and commitment. May we pray to God to always be giving us a heart of contentment

> *[6] but godliness with contentment is great gain,*
> *[7] for we brought nothing into the world, and[a] we cannot take anything out of the world*
> *[8] but if we have food and clothing, with these we will be content.*
> *[9] but those who desire to be rich fall into temptation, into a snare, into many senseless and harmful desires that plunge people into ruin and destruction.*
> *[10] For the love of money is a root of all kinds of evils. It is through this craving that some have wandered away from the faith and pierced themselves with many pangs.*

**1 Timothy 6:6-12**

Back to my studies progress, after my high school studies, I joined an all girl college for my IT studies. My life in college was great as I had transitioned from primary and high school education. I worked hard and I maintained discipline as I schooled in an environment where the institution was run by the catholic sisters. I was in very remote area because my parents felt the need to protect me from the world. I made friends and relations that would continue many years later even as we pursue our careers.

I avoided any activity that will divert me from achieving my education goals. I never partied or involved myself to what many girls of my age would engage. I was not adventurous just yet. I was able to focus on my faith and this cushioned me of the exposures of campus life. I was a darling to the nuns, and would always get a chance to sing the psalms in church.

In his first letter to the Corinthians, the apostle Paul wrote of the false teacher's. Those people who only consider their physical existence and as a result, their moral outlook on life becomes questionable.

Paul is telling us that in associating with false teachers, we will be adversely influenced by them. *"Bad company corrupts good character"* (**1 Corinthians 15:33**). The truth is that false teachings do not lead to good life. As such, it is critical that we are careful whom we form relationships with; especially those who mislead us because they can cause even the strongest believers to waver in their faith and adversely affect their walk with Christ and their witness to the world. This is why Paul tells us, *"Do not be misled."*

In **1 Corinthians 6:9**, Paul cautioned them not to take up the lifestyles of corrupt people those who will not inherit the kingdom of God. Paul knew how easy it is for people to be influenced by such adverse teachings. If not checked at the very beginning, they could begin to adopt such perverted ideas and behaviors as normal.

When we associate with or take delight in the company of people with worldly morals, we run the risk of mimicking their behaviors, their language, and their habits. Before long we are no longer of Christ, but of the world with its denial of absolute authority, its rejection of the Bible as the Word of God, and its ideology of relative morality. This is especially pertinent to young people who are generally easily influenced by their peers. Young people are desperate for the approval of others. So motivated are they by the need for acceptance that godly wisdom in decision making can go out the window in the face of peer pressure. Therefore, it is crucial for parents of young teens especially to be on guard against the influence of bad company.

> *"Therefore, my dear brothers, stand firm.*
> *Let nothing move you. Always give yourselves fully to the work of the Lord, because you know that your labor in the Lord is not in vain"*
> ***1 Corinthians 15:58***

In my college years, my strong faith in Christ helped shape my character and helped me to be focused on my studies. I came out of the institution with much success as I graduated with BSc (IT) second class upper division. The sky was the limit in my future endeavors.

So what should we do to withstand bad teachings and bad characters in our lives? As parents, we stand firm against ungodly influences that may corrupt our children. As Christians, we stand firm against those who would corrupt our walk with Christ. As church members, we stand firm against false teaching and watered-down gospel presentations that lead others astray. In all things, we are *"self-controlled and alert"* because our *"enemy the devil prowls around like a roaring lion looking for someone to devour"* (**1 Peter 5:8**).

# 3

# Life Changing Morning

It's a joy for every young person after graduating to join the job market and thrive. God graciously honored me with that opportunity. I joined an IT company in 2006 for my first employment at the age of 23. That was a beautiful opportunity for me. The girl from the slopes of mount Kenya is now on the path of making it in the big city. My future looked glorious, but it was short lived on this dreadful morning.

I had rented a small house far from the office, which was an achievement for me. I used to wake up early and be on the road by 5.00am in the morning.

It was on a Monday morning in the month of December, I had woken up as usual with the energy of starting off a new week. Prepared myself as the custom of a 23 year old beautiful girl. Worn my best look and after breakfast I started my early morning journey to the bus station. I didn't know that my life would change at that very moment for the rest of my life and Yes my life took a totally different turn.

As I was walking along the road towards the bus stop to make it to the office on time, I met three men on the road  and as they passed me instantly they turned and one of them hit me with a blunt object on my head. That hit landed me on the ground. They held me, lifted me up to a secluded place near the road and the worst happened. By this time i was confused, in pain, I was lost, I couldn't shout, I was completely not myself. That head hit had suspended my mind completely. In this space of confusion they raped me in turns, They robbed me of everything I had in my bag; and the most precious thing I had held so dear to myself. They robbed me of my innocence and my virginity and left me for dead.

After regaining consciousness, in my state of confusion, pain and hopelessness, I ran to a nearby pub and met people who sympathized with me.

At this instant, God had positioned people on my path that would be used by Him to hold my hand to stand again. It looked obvious to me by then, but today I know it's God who had positioned them there.

There was this taxi driver who offered to accompany me to the police station where we reported the incident. By this time I didn't know if crying was the right thing to respond to what I felt or to shout in agony. The joyful girl who came to the big city with big dreams and goals was now no more. I felt different in all ways. I felt it was all lost and I couldn't put all this pieces together. ***Why am I going through this? Who did I wrong? Why now? Do I really deserve this?*** All these questions were flooding my mind.

I was advised to visit the women hospital in Hurlingham which is a known hospital for rape victims.

It was at the hospital that the reality of the whole ordeal played before me. After I narrated what happened, I saw a file being opened for GENDER BASED VIOLENCE VICTIMS and my name was about to get a number in that book. I cried my heart out. The pain I felt was like a red hot sharp arrow going through my flesh and heart. As the Nurse asked my name, and she was writing it in the book, each Letter I saw her write pushed the Red hot sharp arrow deeper into my flesh. The S U S A N  K I B E each letter was a pain In itself. The pain of re-telling my story at every point from administration to the nurses was overwhelming. Each re-telling was like I was being raped over and over again. I was in turmoil.

I wanted people to understand me. To understand my innocence in all what I was going through. The pain in my heart was so much that there was nothing on the outside that would quench it or reduce it even in the slightest way.

The trauma of being raped or sexually assaulted is life shattering, leaving you feeling scared, dirty, ashamed, and alone or plagued by nightmares, flashbacks, and other unpleasant memories. It's an ordeal I can't wish for even my worst enemy.

In that state of agony and horrible pain, God had positioned an angel just to minister to this girl who was at her breaking point. She was a counselor working at the Women hospital, and that morning she had reported to work as was the norm. This morning she had a mandate to Minister to me. Her name is Penina.

***God bless her for me specifically.***

She counseled me with the best words that I had ever listened to. In her own words she said, "*Susan, today you are only 23 years old. If only God will give you 70 years to live, you should decide how the rest of your 47 years will be. The rape incident this morning is not written on your forehead but your future will be determined by how you will write it. On how you will live the rest of 47 years of your life that God has prepared ahead of you if we only work with 70 years mortality rate. The life ahead of you is greater than all what you have gone through. You are a strong woman and the best years lay ahead of you*".

She continued to say that "*no matter how bad you feel right now, it's important to remember that you weren't to blame for what happened and you can regain your sense of safety and trust.*"

Those words were so comforting in the midst of the pain I was in. Those words were holy spirit breathed. They were comforting and they made me realize that am still in charge of my life

### To anyone who has been through sexual assault

If you've been raped or assaulted, you dont have to go through this alone. Remember its not your fault. You may be feeling a range of emotions, but whatever you feel, know that what happened wasn't your fault. It was 100% their fault. Dont blame yourself for anything you did or didn't do.

Make sure you're safe. Get to a safe place or call a friend who can help you. If you're in immediate danger, call 911. If the person who assaulted you is a family member or someone you know, tell someone you trust what happened.

Once you're in a safe place, dont do anything to change your appearance. You don't have to decide right away if you're going to talk with the police about what happened or press charges against the person who assaulted you. But just in case you do, its important that the doctor or nurse you visit can collect any evidence that might be on your body. So don't take a shower or bath or wash off any parts of your body. Also if you can, don't go to the bathroom, comb your hair, eat, drink or take any drugs. If you change your clothes, take the clothes you were wearing during the assault to the hospital or police department in a paper bag.

Get medical care. If you have injuries, or want to have a rape test done to collect evidence in case you decide to file charges someday, you should go to the hospital right away.

If you're worried about having been exposed to HIV, you can take a medicine called PEP (post exposure prophylaxis) which can help prevent getting HIV after being exposed. You need to start this treatment within 72 hours of being exposed.

If there's a chance you could be pregnant, consider taking the morning-after pill, also known as emergency contraceptive. You need to take it within 5 days after unprotected sex.

If you're worried about STDs, its a good idea to get tested. Most people don't show any symptoms, so even if you dont have any signs of an STD, testing is important.

It is always important to find support. Dealing with the aftermath of rape or sexual assault can be overwhelming. But you're not alone. It may help to talk to a trusted friend, family member, or counselor.

Think about talking to the police. Sexual assault is a crime and you have the right to report it to the police and press charges against the person who assaulted you if you want to. You can call the police yourself, or have a rape crisis counselor or someone you trust do it for you. The police will come and ask you questions, and they'll also talk to you about whether or not you want to press charges. Police can also help get you to a doctor or nurse for an exam as soon as possible. The decision to call the police or not, is yours to make.

The only time this isn't true is if you are a minor *(younger than the age of consent in your state)* and you tell someone like a teacher, counselor, or doctor who is a mandated reporter. This means that they have to call the police no matter if you want them to or not, according to laws that protect minors.

There is always help, if you reach out for it.

# 4

## Picking Myself Up

Only God can comfort a broken heart.
Only God can heal a sick heart.
Only God can lift a shattered heart.

I acknowledge God as the only one who bounced me back. He never let my hand go even when I felt all alone and lost.

Recovering from sexual trauma takes time, and the healing process can be painful. But with the right strategies and support, you can move past the trauma, rebuild your sense of control and self-worth, and even come out the other side feeling stronger and more resilient.

I received the best treatment from the hospital and I thank God that after running all the tests, the results were negative.

After getting all the treatment and getting all the support that I needed, I headed back home. I was given medication to carry home.

My journey back home and in a public bus was my lowest moment ever. I call it my darkest journey yet I was walking during the day. I would see people walking, smiling laughing and I would beg them with stares to understand my situation. How come everyone is okay and am not okay?

I wanted everyone to know that I have been robbed of my innocence. Regardless of age or gender, the impact of what I had been through went far beyond any physical injuries. I wished they had broken my leg, I would be in a plaster for a few weeks And heal. How do I heal from a broken heart? How do I make this nightmare roll away?

The world didn't feel like a safe place anymore. I lost Trust with everyone I met. I couldn't even trust myself. I questioned my judgment, my self-worth, and even my sanity. I blamed myself for what happened.

When I arrived home, I called my then boyfriend who really sympathized with me and supported me fully. I also called my office to notify them of my ordeal and to give me time to heal. I was still in shock, I felt like I wasn't safe even in my own house. That night I rolled on my bed in anguish and emptiness. I wished I would delete that day from my life and never remember it. I wished I woke up late and gotten to work late than waking up to meet those men on my way to work. I wished I didn't have that job that made me wake up that early.

That very night my mum couldn't wait for morning to come for her to travel to the city to come and console her only daughter. It was equally hard on her. Early in the morning there was a knock at my door and my beautiful mother stood at the door step. When I opened my door for her, her little baby girl fell into her arms and I cried like a small baby. In her arms I was vulnerable. Those were the safest arms I had ever known that even in my worst those arms were always open for me to fall at. It was an intense moment of emotions and sobbing. We both hugged and cried so much. My mum felt hurt that after taking care of me for all those years, this had happened to me. It was a painful moment for both of us.

She would later take me to Kikuyu Hospital for eye check up as I had been injured in my eyes during the rape incidence. Mum stayed with me for a couple of days. She helped me heal as sometimes I would look at the drugs the hospital gave me and wonder how I got myself in to this.

After staying with mum for few days, she would later with the help of my family and my aunt help me move to my aunties place at Nairobi west as I decided my next move. Aunt Sarah (Nairobi West) may God continue to bless you and generations for the kind gesture you showed me. I received the needed support from my family who never questioned my character. They always loved me unconditionally and this helped me heal in a great way.

I later came to learn that when a person goes through such an incident as rape; their expectations are that everyone will understand the predicament. I was wrong. I felt different from my place of work. I never received the support that I needed. No follow up calls to check on how I was doing. No material support or visit and I felt annoyed with my place of work. I felt they let me down as the incident had happened on my way to work. I felt like they should have done more.

I reported back to work but few days in the office I felt that I didn't have the strength to face the same people who knew me and what I had gone through every morning. I felt like my presence around them was bringing me shame.

After settling with my auntie at Nairobi west, I stopped going to work and started looking for another job. I later got employed by Barclays bank in 2007 to sell Barclaycard and I would later move to Kileleshwa to live on my own.

## Walking With a Victim

Rape or sexual assault can be a traumatic, life-changing event. Sadly, chances are that you will come across somebody who has experienced it during the course of your life. We are all surrounded by people who have gone through traumatic situations. Instances like loss of loved one, Rape, accident, divorce and many other instances. These people need help from people they can trust. So how can we help a person who has gone through a traumatic experience?

For instances like in rape, we should listen and believe them. We should remind them that they're not alone. Dont judge or blame them for what happened. Remember that the blame is on the person who commits the assault, and not on the victim. Tell the person you believe them.

The most important thing you can do is let them know that you believe what they are telling you. Too often, victims are greeted with statements like, **are you sure?** Instead, tell them, I believe you. I hear what you are saying.

Its really difficult for most people to tell someone about abuse. Resist the urge to ask the rape victim for details, such as what happened and who did it. Make sure that your friend knows you are there for them and not to satisfy your own curiosity. It can be difficult to know how to help someone you love and care for when they have gone through a distressing or frightening event.

Its natural to want to make someone you love and care for feel better again, but its important to accept what has happened. There is nothing you can say or do to make the persons pain disappear. That will happen with time, rest, and appropriate support. Explain to them that you are sorry about what they have had to experience and that you are there to help them in any way they need. We should offer support after a traumatic or distressing event. Its always good to ask the person who has experienced a traumatic or distressing event what you can do to support them.

**Suggestions for supporting a friend or family member include:**

Make time to be with the person and make it obvious that you are available. Sometimes, there can be a tendency to expect them to move on before they are ready, because the traumatic experience makes us feel uncomfortable. Try to avoid doing this. People who have had a traumatic experience can feel very reassured by human contact.

Don't take their feelings to heart. They may be irritable, depressed, angry or frightened. Strong feelings and emotional outbursts are common, try not to take it personally. It is important to recognize that they have had a stressful experience and that their reactions are normal and will subside with time. You can help by reassuring the person that their reactions are normal. Offer practical support. You could do the housework or the grocery shopping for them, or pick up their children from school.

Encourage the person to take good care of themselves, for example, by eating well, avoiding alcohol, drugs or stimulants, and by attempting to maintain regular sleeping habits. You may need to let the person have time by themselves. Let them know you are there for them without judging. Suggesting to a person that they maintain regular daily routines and habits can be helpful as well. Keep asking your friend to do things. Dont assume that your friend no longer wants to do anything fun. Keep inviting them to do things like take a walk or go to a movie.

Take care of your own needs. Comforting your friend is important, but it can also be really difficult. You'll likely deal with your own wide range of emotions, such as frustration and anxiety. Remember to be kind to yourself. Spend time with other friends, make sure your own needs are met, and seek counseling for yourself if necessary.

I can relate very well to the above on how people around you can help you ease the pain after a traumatic incidence. This is what happened to me. My friends helped me feel loved and cared for during that season of healing.

# 5

# The Impact of Abuse

After the assault and gradual healing, I recall that I felt shattered. I felt incomplete. Surviving a rape encounter is a traumatic experience that impacts its victims in a physical, psychological, and sociological way. Even though the effects and aftermath of rape differ among survivors, individuals tend to suffer from similar issues found within these three categories.

Long term reactions may involve the development of coping mechanisms that will either benefit the survivor, such as social support, or inhibit their recovery. Seeking support and professional resources may assist the survivor in numerous ways.

I later came to learn that, in the journey of life, most people will experience a trauma at some point in their lives, and as a result, some will experience debilitating symptoms that interfere with daily life. Those suffering from post traumatic stress can have trouble functioning in their jobs or personal relationships. For me, I had trouble in my work place. I felt out of place. I could not concentrate on my work. For children affected by post-traumatic stress, they can have difficulty in school, become isolated from others and develop phobias. Many people with Post Traumatic Stress Disorder repeatedly re-experience the ordeal in the form of flashback episodes, memories, nightmares, or frightening thoughts, especially when they are exposed to events or objects that remind them of the trauma. Post traumatic Stress Disorder is diagnosed when these symptoms last more than one month.

In general, cognitive-behavioral therapies which strive to help traumatized individuals understand and manage the anxiety and fear they are experiencing prove to be effective in producing significant reductions in Post Traumatic Stress Disorder symptoms in rape survivors. Specialized interventions help in effectively preventing PTSD in some trauma patients.

One of the cognitive-behavioral treatments that I received at the Nairobi women's hospital which lasted several sessions included cognitive restructuring techniques for replacing catastrophic, self-defeating thought patterns with more adaptive, self-reassuring statements. As I had stated in the earlier chapter, one of the counselors at the hospital emphasized that rape incidence should not stop me from carrying on with my life. This is one of the cognitive treatments that helped me in my healing journey. It is said that cognitive therapy if used within a few weeks of exposure to traumas, this brief form of therapy often prevents PTSD in survivors of both sexual and nonsexual assaults.

In addition to targeted, brief interventions, some trauma survivors may benefit from ongoing counseling or treatment, those who benefit from such treatment include survivors with a history of previous trauma, survivors of the current trauma who have a history of childhood physical or sexual abuse or those who have pre-existing mental health problems.

In my case, the Nairobi women's Hospital staff continued with counselling and followed up on my situation for 6 months something that helped me feel strong. I thank God for my family and the hospital that I didn't experience too much Post Traumatic Stress.

Despite the follow up from the hospital and emotional healing, deep inside me, I was still hurting. I started partying heavily as I wanted to forget my situation. I was bitter with the world. I couldn't understand why I had preserved myself without engaging in premarital sex only to be assaulted at my prime age. Partying was my way of running away from bitterness. There is a certain rush that comes from running away from our problems and issues surrounding us. We tend to liberate ourselves from issues using our own strength. We forget to involve God in our thoughts and actions. We tend to liberate ourselves.

We cannot face all issues in our lives with intensity and passion needed as quickly as we can. We do not possess the patience or perspective that is needed to arrive at our solutions, so we instead take the easy way out, we run away.

After the incident, I became afraid to love anything or anyone fully. I couldn't live anywhere completely neither could I invest myself entirely in anything new. I wanted to forget the simple girl that I was and embrace the new me; party girl. I felt that my problems didn't exist here in this new physical place that I had arrived at.

When you run away from all of your problems, you eventually start tripping. The things you're running from dont explicitly appear in front of you but linger just beneath your mind's surface cooing taunts at your newest undertakings.

The problem with running away is that we try as much as possible to define a solution to an ongoing problem. We are attempting to tie up the loose threads of our lives before we've detangled any of them. We all want resolutions as simple as purchasing a plane ticket, updating our current City on Facebook and moving on with our lives, but we forget that our emotional ties run deeper than that. We forget that we can never fly far enough away from ourselves to escape what it is that lies unresolved within us.

Our issues are not left in the places we leave behind or the people we no longer see every day. Our unresolved emotional clutter seeps into every phase of our lives, silently enough to remain eternally undetected. Its the sense of self-doubt that creeps in when we are challenged. Its the same old pain of trying to write a new chapter without finishing the old one. You do not have a frame of reference to carry on forward. You're trying to grab at something new with full hands and yet you cannot figure out why you keep dropping it.

*Numbing the pain for a while will*
*Make it worse when you finally feel it,*
*J.K. Rowling*

It is true that pain can be avoided almost entirely but the bleakness that accompanies the pain cannot. When you constantly run from the past, it wears away the present with a vengeance. You become afraid to love anything fully, live anywhere completely, and invest yourself entirely in any new person or venture, for the underlying fear that eventually you are going to fail, that you aren't going to stick around when the going gets tough.

That you'll be gone and with you will fade all of the sweet, unfinished memories, all of the plans, all of the careful devotions that you promised with uncertain lips.

When you're the person who runs away from everything, you dont get to be fully present anywhere. You know you wont be staying so you check out. You check out from everything that makes you alive.

When you run away from all of your problems, you eventually run from yourself. You forget the person you could be if you stayed in one place, worked through your downfalls, accepted your shortcomings and then overcome them. You forget that there's a version of you who is reliable and passionate and strong. You lose the sense of pride you used to have from persevering.

When you run away from all of your problems, you run right into infinitely more. You create a world within yourself that must be tiptoed through and gets over-turned with ease. You are a land mine of unfinished wounds that bleed again at the slightest scratch. You find yourself having to constantly run farther, harder, faster, to avoid what you are carrying within yourself. The farther you run from your problems, the farther you run from yourself. And the harder it becomes to eventually find your way back home.

Even though my then boyfriend never abandoned me, I felt hatred in my heart. I vowed to heal and bounce back but this time, I didn't want to play the innocent girl, and I wanted another life.

# 6

## Broken Piece

### *The birth of my first born*

Days transitioned into months and by now, I was no longer the Susan kibe that I was before. I took on a don't care attitude and my life style changed completely. All I wanted was to get away from that feeling of emptiness but I didn't know the best way how. So I ended up being a parting girl.

Each weekend, was my time to join my girl friends and we would go partying. Life looked awesome but deep in me I was horrible.

In between partying and the age of 25, I conceived my son with my boyfriend. This got me unprepared and I was in awe. I was in complete denial. This is not what I had envisioned in my life when I was a little girl. I had pictured myself getting married in church surrounded by my family. I had seen myself walking down the aisle in a big cathedral with a long cathedral gown sweeping the entire aisle behind me as my dad walked me down the aisle.

I had envisioned my dowry ceremony and my entire village gathering to celebrate with us. I had envisioned me being the best example to other young girls in the village of what it means to have a perfect life.

I had desired to raise my children in a complete home. With a father and mother present. That perfect family I had in my dreams but in the reality things were happening differently.

This is not what I had bargained for. At 25 pregnant No! I couldn't imagine it was happening but unfortunately or fortunately it was happening.

At that moment and time, I felt that all my life expectations and plans were not coming together. But hello!, God's plan is not our plan. Many times we plan everything in our lives without knowing that God's plan prevails.

> **Proverbs 19:21** *states that;*
> *"Many are the plans in a man's heart, but it is the LORD's purpose that prevails."*

I could only see my life plans failing but I didn't realize that God was passing me through His plans. He had it all figured out.

In the Bible, God talks of how He has a plan for each and every person He created.

> *"For I know the plans I have for you, declares the Lord,*
> *Plans to prosper you, but not to harm you*
> *Plans to give you a hope and a future"*
> **Jeremiah 29:11**

God has a plan for every person. I used to hear those words countless times growing up. When I was younger and heard that phrase, I often thought that I would one day wake up *"all grown up"*, and I would know what God's plan for me was.

However, I would later mature and come to learn that this is not so. Back then when I was young, seven out of seven days a week you are under the control of someone when you are a child. Whether it's a parent or a teacher, you are expected to obey the set rules. I believe that obeying God and being in his plans has a great role in God's plan for our lives. We all learn many things from being guided by our parents. Therefore, I believe that God's plan for your life starts with the day you were born.

There are two ways I interpret the phrase *"God has a plan for your life"*. The first way, is that I read that phrase with the future in mind. For example, when I was young, I used to think of the future. I would think of who I will marry, where I will live, where I will go to college, what will I major in, and many other things. I often wondered where God will take me in the future.

The second way I interpret the phrase *"God has plan for your life"* is on a much more detailed scale. I believe God has a purpose for everything that happens. For example, that morning when I realized that I was pregnant with my first born child, I was afraid. After all, that I have gone through and now this? *"Really! God? Well, today I believe that it didn't "just happen"*. Maybe God was trying to teach me a little something about patience or slowing down in life.

What about the time that the waiter spills tea all over a person with a new shirt? Could that really happen for a reason? Well, yes. God might have allowed the person to sit at the table with the clumsiest waitress in the restaurant to help teach him a little thing about forgiveness, or being slow to anger.

God places issues in our lives and allows us to go through situations that will help us in the future. So every time something happens to me I think about what God might be trying to teach me. After all, He does have a plan for my life. Despite the fears and doubts in my situation, I carried my child to full term with no complications and this gave me joy to know that God wanted to give my child the best in life.

The birth of my son was welcomed by everyone at home with open arms, my parents and my siblings. Being the first grandchild in our family, he meant a lot to my parents.

However, my world changed the time I gave birth to my son. I started fearing how I will raise my child in a single parent home contrary to how I grew up with both parents. I came to realize that the role of a single parent is very demanding and challenging. The most evident challenge faced by a single parent is to be the sole provider for his/her children. Commonly, a single parent is the only bread winner of the entire household and is, therefore, unable to give more time to the children due to work pressure. On the other hand, other families having both parents taking responsibility of their family not only earn dual income but also are able to manage their time such that one of the parents, at least, is always available to take care and monitor the children. Single parents are deprived of this privilege. Other challenges that the single parent has to cope with include acquiring child support. Due to these challenges and issues, single parents struggle to have real family fun and entertainment.

My family was very supportive in helping me raise my son and even though the father of my child helped me to raise the baby, he stopped in a year or so and I found myself being the sole provider for my baby. However, I didn't want to beg for support from his father.

Even though I had changed to a better paying job at Britam, the bills were too high for me and my son. I had been used to feed one person but here I was with a young one. I was still in denial now that I was a single parent.

Even after the birth of my son, and the difference it made in my life, it never took the void I felt in me. So I continued partying. I was looking for something to fill the emptiness in me and because I couldn't find it, going out and drinking gave me temporary satisfaction. With my now okay salary I managed to keep that lifestyle as a cover up. Because that life was not me. Partying gave me Happiness for a moment and that was okay with me.

# 7

## Counterfeit in Marriage

When my son was 4 years old, I met this gentleman and in a flash I started dating him. By this time I was still hoping and dreaming to have a perfect home. And so that drove me into his arms. Without much thinking. All I wanted was to settle down in a marriage to raise my son in a *"complete"* family set up.

I believed in marriage, putting in mind I grew up seeing my mum and dad portraying a good example, and I really desired to settle down.

As much as that's what I wanted I didn't have much revelation about it. The bible says that God instituted marriage with the first man and woman, Adam and Eve.

> *"Therefore shall a man leave his father and his mother, and shall cleave unto his wife: and they shall be one flesh"*
> **(Gen. 2:20-24)**

There are three factors delineated for a marriage union. The *"leaving"* delineates the social factor, the *"cleaving"* delineates the spiritual factor. All these factors are necessary to constitute a Biblical marriage. The social factor involves a public awareness that the couple is married. This awareness is usually conveyed by a public ceremony or document. The spiritual factor involves a unity of mind and heart on the major matters of life. It culminates into the covenant that God is present in. The sexual factor involves an intimate relationship which is monogamous and permanent. These factors are foundational and prerequisite for strong family units for any society. It is obvious that some Bible characters were polygamous, but God's plan is nevertheless binding for all who desire the Lord's blessing for strong families. In the New Testament, Christ reaffirmed this marriage formula for His audience. He answered,

*"Have you not read that he who created them from the beginning made them male and female, and said, 'Therefore a man shall leave his father and his mother and hold fast to his wife, and the two shall become one flesh'? So they are no longer two but one flesh. What therefore God has joined together let not man separate."*

All this I didn't know. I just wanted a man in my life and a father in the life of my son. But I didn't have a clue what this entailed in the mind of God.

My mind was settled on getting married at all cost. I stopped partying and started focusing on settling down like other girls of my age. I was preparing myself for marriage. My new boyfriend introduced me to church and I became a born again Christian. This gave me a new lease of life. This looked perfect for me. The image I had in my mind and heart over the years was becoming a reality right infront of me.

I would later settle with my boyfriend in an arrangement, and this is when I conceived my daughter.

In as much as I was delighted to have my daughter, I couldn't face my family. I hid my pregnancy from my parents and siblings because I felt that I had let them down. I gave birth to my daughter in December 2013.

I was not happy with the decision to stay together with my boyfriend without having a church wedding but again my daughter gave me much joy as a mother. All children are a gift from God. Every single life, every single child, is a reward and blessing. Whether they're bringing parents pride and joy, or whether they are teaching us how to be more patient and forgiving, children are a gift from God and a source for the growth of His Kingdom here on Earth.

God knows that children can bring us closer to Him and help grow our Christian character.

Settling down with my boyfriend gave my children a complete family set up. My prayer was answered. I enjoyed going to church with my children and my husband and I became steadfast in prayers.

I started trusting God with my life again. Not just to believe in who He is and what He says; I was confident in the perfect plan He had for me and my children. I trusted Him with my life and that of my children.

> *Trust in the Lord with all your heart, and do not lean on your own understanding. In all your ways acknowledge him, and he will make straight your paths.* **Proverbs 3:5-6**

All of our knowledge, wisdom, and will should be saturated in the action-producing assurance of the Lord. When we lean on our own understanding, we trust our own knowledge and discernment to support us through life.

### The problem with this is that
*"the heart is deceitful above all things, and desperately sick; who can understand it?"*
Jeremiah 17:9

### Our own sinful nature can't be counted on.
But new hearts are given by Christ through the Holy Spirit. We cultivate God-trusting hearts by meditating on Scripture, time in prayer, and companionship with other believers. As these things tune our hearts to the Spirit living in us, we will rely less on ourselves and more on Christ, serving him in good times and bad, in sickness and in health, in the battle with sin and in the peace of his rest.

To trust is to acknowledge God in everything. Acknowledging God means knowing God wherever we are and in whatever we are doing. This doesn't just mean intellectual assent, but an act of perceiving his character and will in every moment of life. When we dedicate ourselves to trusting and seeking God in all circumstances, we should not assume that life will be easy and that no trouble will befall us.

My past life experiences taught me that trusting God and acknowledging him will make our lives not to be shaken when trials come.
*Blessed is the man who trusts in the Lord,*
*whose trust is the Lord.*
*He is like a tree planted by water,*

*that sends out its roots by the stream,*
*and does not fear when heat comes,*
*for its leaves remain green,*
*and is not anxious in the year of drought,*
*for it does not cease to bear fruit.*
**Jeremiah 17:7-8**

It's not that life no longer has difficulties when we trust God, but that those difficulties are nothing to fear and that we can remain confident in God in the midst of them. He keeps us vibrant and useful to his will even when we feel languished or that the times are against us.

As we trust more in Jesus and have confidence to act on his will, we may have to turn down opportunities that seem great because Jesus has called us elsewhere, or accept callings that scare us.

Acknowledging God in everything means that we remember that no circumstances come to us outside of the Father's will. Knowing this will give us strength even through difficulties, pains, and fears, because we know that God will never leave our side. I prayed to God for direction to settle in marriage and in life.

My second year in marriage, God revealed to me that what I was praying for, He could only do it in one way, if I trusted him.

I had a lot in my mind. I used to ask myself, where am I with my children? What have I done to find myself where I am?

I started attending New Breed Chapel consistently and it is at that time and season that I started getting help from reading the bible and seeking counsel from my pastor regarding my *"marriage"* and my life.

## Separation

In my 3rd year in the arrangement, I decided to step out and allow God to settle me *"Himself"*. I realized that my *"husband"* and I had no purpose in life together. We separated amicably with him.

This was one of my hardest decision as a believer as people viewed us as a perfect couple. I didn't label my partner as a bad person or bad mouth him to the children as this is ungodly and also I am the one who felt that we are not living in Gods purpose together.

Every marriage should have a reason for its existence. For many people, marriage is for love and companionship. It's something that you do because you want to be a part of your partner's life, and you want your partner to be part of yours.

However, marriage is also a legal union. When you get married, many aspects of your life become entwined -finances, parental responsibilities, insurance, schedules, and many other aspects. As a result, some people get married because they feel like they have to, whether for legal reasons or societal or religious reasons like raising a child together.

You need to know whether the primary reasons for your marriage are found in love and companionship, other benefits, or some combination of the two. Usually, it's the last one. People get married out of love and then find that it's much easier and more enjoyable to get by on two incomes, to share responsibilities, and raise a family with a partner. There are many alternative ways to find satisfaction and purpose in a marital relationship. Further, these ways often change as the relationship and its members change. Another huge reason behind getting married is creating a stable family within which to raise children. And all those other reasons - emotional, legal, societal, and financial - affect the lives of the child or children that you and your partner may have together. That's why when you consider the purpose of your marriage, you need to think about all the different reasons and determine their priority in your relationship.

Ideally, you had an idea of why you wanted to get married to your partner before living together. But if you are already several months or years into your union and wondering why you are there, you may need to re-define the purpose of your marital relationship. Don't look at this as a problem with the relationship; look at it as an opportunity to find purpose in your life.

Finding purpose in your marital relationship can take two main forms. The first of these is rediscovering your purpose. The second is defining a new purpose for your marital relationship.

Rediscovering the purpose for your marital relationship is common in relationships that are still fairly young or in couples that have had some hardship. As I mentioned above, you probably had a reason for marrying your partner in the first place. However, if you have been very busy or life has been more difficult than you expected, you can forget what that purpose was. There are new feelings more enjoyable than remembering what that reason was and discovering those emotions again. Some people can do this by just talking to their partner about their early relationship or going through photo albums. Others may try to revisit places where you once visited or do activities that you once enjoyed, but this doesn't work for everyone.

Defining a new purpose can be necessary for people who have been married longer, who married younger, or who have been through other significant changes together. In these cases, you may have had reasons for getting married, but now those reasons may not seem to apply anymore. That doesn't mean that your marriage is necessarily over but to give your marriage a priority you should try to determine what its purposes are, now that you and the relationship have changed or matured.

It makes sense if you think about it: you're not the same person that you were when you got married and if the marriage isn't changing with you, what good is it? Just like rediscovering your purpose for your marital relationship can be very rewarding, deciding what it means to you in new stages of your life can be like falling in love all over again. Some couples can do this by talking about the things that they need from the relationship or how the relationship meets their needs even if these cases have changed since the relationship began.

## Finding Your Purpose

Because the purpose of your marital relationship is to have a team mate who helps you in reaching your own goals, you need to know what your purpose is for your spouse to support you in that. And support for life goals is an important purpose for marriage to serve. Other friends and family can also offer support as you reach for your goals, but your spouse is usually the person who is with you the most. For most of us, there are also things that we can tell our spouses that we wouldn't want to share with other friends and family members.

Marriage should not take away your purpose. And seeking out your own goals and growing towards them is one of the best ways to live a purpose driven life.

Having individual goals that you can support each other towards creates a balanced relationship where each of you can continue to learn about the other throughout the long-term. That means you should also be supportive of your partner's goals and endeavors. If there is an opposite to the problem of not knowing what the purpose of a relationship between individuals is, that opposite does not know what the purpose of individuals is outside of the relationship. It can be all too easy to forget that the person sleeping next to you is more than just your spouse; they are their complete person.

If you find your marriage lacking meaning, your partner doesn't seem receptive to supporting you in your individual goals, or you're having difficulty supporting your spouse, tell them. This can be a difficult discussion to have. You may be afraid that you will hurt your partner's feelings by saying that you aren't sure about the purpose of the relationship. Many people also feel defensive, believing that they are having these problems because they are somehow weak or failures.

If you are worried about how your partner will take it, just take it slowly and explain yourself. Tell them that you still love them and value the relationship. Let the know that you feel like it could mean more to you, and that you want to make it stronger.

If you are worried about what your partner will think of you, it should be the least of your concerns since marriage makes you one. Your partner should be there to support you, especially if you are worried about the relationship. Further, most people go through this kind of phase at least once in their relationship. Relationships grow and change and the people in them grow and change. Wanting to understand and define your marital relationship doesn't mean that you are doing something wrong or even that there is something wrong with your relationship. In my case, we were presenting ourselves all through as a perfect couple and this confused our friends especially in church as they could not understand. I had all along hidden my private life and private battles ad I prayed God for strength to bear it all. I was very strong in public but hurting in private.

My partner would later relocate to a different town and this made the separation easier. I learnt once again to raise my two children on my own but with God behind the scenes of our lives. I became a more prayerful person and always consulted God about my children.

I transitioned from *"marriage"* life to again being single and this was one of my hardest seasons in life. I separated from someone I had gotten used to, my friend and my confidant. The person my children knew as a father.

> 5 *God is father to the fatherless, a defender of widows,*
>    *is God in his holy dwelling.*
> 6 *God sets the lonely in families,[a]*
>    *he leads out the prisoners with singing;*
>
>    *but the rebellious live in a sun-scorched land.*
> **Psalm 68:5-6 (NIV)**

# 8

# The Call

At the lowest point of my young adult life, I had to make a decision that would affect me many years ahead. God had a lot in store for me. I chose to be positive and face life smiling, amidst my pain. Understanding and Discovering God's will for my life was based on **Isaiah 43:1**. *"Do not fear, for I have redeemed you; I have summoned you by name; you are mine"*. The verse provided great insight into the trust; guidelines and changes that I needed to seek and discover God's will for my life.

Looking back, I could see God was preparing me for ministry. What pushed me was that I needed to be clear in order to be in ministry. God needed me either to be with him or the world. I needed to clear the grey areas in my life.

I believe that marriage works as it was instituted by God. I also believe that divorce is not final, finding God's purpose is what matters in life. I was glad that the church accepted me the way I was.

My family supported me in all my decisions at that time. Rev Vicky Mwangi of New Breed Chapel used to tell me that the situation will, *'make me a better person but not a bitter person'*. She would tell me that if God had allowed this season in my life for ministry to be born, then I should just allow it. The advice was not easy to take, I felt like she did not understand me, but I had submitted my life to counsel and authority so I received it.

At times God will allow us to take a certain path for his own glory. I would question my decisions at that time. I would receive countless questions from my children. But I learnt to answer to every question according to how they would understand better.

In the midst of all that, a ministry was born out of my season of pain, and the journey I had taken. In life we should never arm-twist God. We end up wasting time in doing so.

I also started counting my blessings. Shifting my focus to what I was grateful for and this was an excellent way to forget my troubles. I started cultivating gratitude which shifted my perspective away from my past worries and fears and this gave me a more positive interaction with the world around me.

I came to realize that any time you find yourself troubled, stop and list things you are grateful for. You might be grateful for your family, your health, a roof over your head, your good memories, or a good opportunity.

*"Delight yourself in the LORD,*
*and he will give you the desires of your heart".*
**Psalms 37:4**

I started discovering God's will in my life. I came to realize that God's ways are beyond our comprehension. God is the infinite Creator while we are created and born of man. But there is an interesting twist to this issue that in his own way, God wants to reveal His ways to us. God wanted to reveal himself to me in a special way. **Deuteronomy 29:29** instructs us that the Lord desires to reveal some important matters to His people. *"The secret things belong to the LORD our God,*

> *But the things revealed belong to us and to our sons forever,*
> *That we may observe all the words of this law"*
> **(Deut 29:29)**

By digging dipper into the word of God, I learnt that the reason we have to walk with God is that we cannot understand God's complete mind, but we can know the thoughts that he has for us.

Every now and then many individuals ask the questions about purpose and meaning of life. Perhaps they have played with their life long enough and have life not as exciting and tantalizing as promised. Material things cannot truly satisfy us but only distract us.

Isn't it true that even if we know about God's ways that we also want to know about our part in it. In fact, as we search the scriptures we will discover that God has a marvelous plan in place.

Although He shows us the entrance to this pathway that leads to fulfillment, we are too often like the spies sent into the Promised Land. Our minds are so cluttered with our thoughts of fulfillment and what it might mean; we never get on that pathway. Or perhaps at some conference we are inspired for a moment to step in that direction but as the vision fades, we find it much more comfortable to walk our old path.

*"You cannot be delivered from what you are still holding"*
**Bishop Erick Mwangi**

God is our source for everything. So please, do not fret, because God will do amazing things in your life. Although the culture we live in always feeds us with worry, doubt and fear, Jesus is the one who holds our future. Power victory, deliverance, freedom is in the name of Jesus. We are a people in transition. During transition, God is more concerned with our condition than our comfort. Seasons of change are crucial. Critical times in our lives.

It is in the whirlwind of transition and turmoil that we find out what we are made of and who is actually in control. I found out whenever I was in charge I ended up in a mess. Even though I wanted the mess fixed, I was afraid to let go for fear it would grow bigger. Well, it is time to let go. When God is in control, even our messes are ordered under His care.

I like to compare letting go with the process of learning to swim. It can be both exhilarating and terrifying. In order to float, allowing the water to hold you up. Only then do you discover the freedom and liberty of swimming. This natural principle reflects a spiritual transition from our natural rule to rule of the Holy Spirit.

The Spirit of the Lord began to minister to me that an angel is on assignment to reverse any hurt and pain from negative relationships and anoint my hands with the blessings of Godly love. The Lord began to minister to me that I had to release my past pain to God for me to get delivered. I kept walking with God. But this would take time as I walked through tough journey.

### Now that I found purpose,

These are some of the questions I've had to answer.

### How did you heal from separation and started living in dignity?

I continued healing from my past by the grace of God. I made up my mind that I want to do things right and to honor God in everything that I was doing. I remember Rev Vicky Mwangi telling me, *"God will not let you down if you honor him"*.

Looking back, I can now clearly see that God held my hand. Being in church helped me in such a big way. The church grounded me and gave me soft landing to rise up again. Rev Vicky and Bishop Erick Mwangi held my hand in every step and they walked with me in every step of my healing.

### My family

My family stood with me too. They supported me in ways I cannot explain. After sharing with my parents on separation, they respected my decision. They said that if the decision is from God, I have their support fully.

Apparently, before I even shared with my mother about the separation decision, she could see that I was not happy in my *"marriage"*. She used to pray for me to know what is good for me and my life. She affirmed her love for me. She helped me to stand strong. God showed her in dreams severally that I was unhappy but she did not know how to approach the topic. Most times matters concerning relationships are not easy to advise about.

**Self development**
In the midst of all this, I started attending self development classes. As life progresses, you are guaranteed to face a variety of circumstances, changing environments, and new roles that require you to adapt to them. A personal development class will help you to handle the pressures that come with the continuous changes and challenges, so that you are well-equipped to excel in all the areas in your life.

Personal development is an ongoing process of self-improvement either in your career, in your education, in your personal life, or in all of these areas. It is about setting goals for you and putting plans in place to reach those goals.

A personal development plan not only helps you to improve on your weaknesses, but it can also help you to develop your strengths. By taking time to focus on nurturing and using your strengths more, you go from being good at something to being excellent at it. You can reach your potential and achieve great growth by developing the skills you are already good at.

Making the decision to improve on your skills takes you a step closer to feeling more confident. Once you have achieved a certain goal, gained another skill, or developed a certain area of your life, you naturally feel good about yourself. The more you keep on developing in the areas of your life you are not confident in, the more you can boost your confidence.

Personal development is closely linked to self-awareness. It gives you the opportunity to take an honest look at the areas of your life that need improvement. Through this process, you get to know who you really are, what your true values are, and where you would like to go in life. Once you go through this process, you will improve your self-awareness and experience fulfillment.

In my case, I attended *"mothers of son"* self development class which is a class that teaches mothers to raise their sons to become the men God intended them to be. To be a successful king, a priest, a worrier, a leader and somebody's future husband. To equip the son with the 4 p's of being a Provider, Protector, Priest and a Prophet. The sons should be raised as the vision carriers of the family. This program taught me intentional parenting, it helped me too heal from my wounds. Healing ensured that I would parent as a whole mum, and not wound my children as well. It was a 10 weeks program that helped me so much on how to raise my son as a single parent. I learnt that if you raise your son through wounded heart he will become a wounded worrier.

I also did **"Noble Womanhood'** which is a program that strengthens women based on **Hebrews 12:12-13.** The lessons teach women to find themselves, understand their family patters and notice what to break from. It was a self-awareness program that helps women find their identity and align to their purpose in God. Going through the program helped me realize that my issues were not unique, I just needed to understand my path and heal. Walking with other women who were also going through their journeys helped to keep moving. I did this program in 12 weeks.

**Self realization**
God was making me go through all this in order to refine me.  I realized that I lacked the guidance as I made decisions earlier. I started the journey of finding myself. After the personal development programs, I started to notice some patterns in my life that were similar to some of my relatives. With the knowledge I had received and the wisdom of the word of God I started to detach myself from patterns I did not like in my family tree. I was discovering myself with each new day.

I was able to shed the self-defeating mentality and focus on what I wanted to achieve. I still needed to settle in marriage *"God's way"*.

I came to realize that when you fall, the decision you make while down there, at that very point, determines how you will rise again. One should not stay in the mud for long. We are taught that God always has a plan. If He closes one door, another one will open and every single thing that happens to us has meaning, a purpose and a lesson.

The events that happen to people are not always fair. I can't tell you how often I've said the words, *"I can't believe that happened to that person. They didn't deserve it."* But I've learned that people who go through the toughest of times are the ones who rise up the highest. Anointing comes from the pressing and that alone kept me going.

When you're knocked down by life hard, the only direction to go is up. A few years ago, one of the greatest fears I had for myself came to pass. My so called perfect life came crashing down around me with very little warning. I was living the life I was raised to believe was the ideal *"married"*, two beautiful children, and a home. None of us think that it will ever happen to us, so when my *"marriage"* ended in separation, I fell into darkness so deep most of my friends and family thought at one time or another I wouldn't make it out.

In my mind and for some time, I was the biggest failure I knew. I believed my family thought I was a complete loser. I was certain that everyone I knew, must be thinking, *"What's wrong with her that she can't have a successful relationship?"*

I was a single mom now and everywhere I went, I carried that identity as a single mum of 2 children. I felt completely overwhelmed at times considering I was emotionally unstable. The lack of a partner day in and day out created the false belief that I couldn't do it by myself. That me and my children were not a, *"real family."* None of this was true of course. They are stories we make up about ourselves to avoid going inward and looking at ourselves and the opportunity we've been given to have something better.

When anything happens that we consider a trauma, whether it is the loss of our job, a business, a relationship, a loved one in our life, or something as unexpected as a terminal illness, there is this amazing opportunity to become real and rise into something greater than where we are.

For me, that failed *"marriage"* meant stripping away of everything I thought I should be and should have in life so I could emerge as who I always was. I stopped pretending to be anything else and started to own all of my mistakes, insecurities and failures. I had to admit that I carried stories about what other people thought of me that simply weren't true.

When we fall hard, most of us feel that we can't get back up. Fear, uncertainty, depression, and the stories that *"we can't"* are what keep us immobilized. We think, *"How am I going to get through this? I'm never going to be happy again."*

You will I promise you. When we fail at something, when we lose everything, we are set free. We are redirected to a new path. One we never saw for ourselves. One we never would have ventured to go down had it not been for the failure.

In my case, I needed to rise fast and heal with my children. I decided to find myself so that I can help my children not to be bitter. I made my son to realize that it is okay to fall and rise again. I had to go through the transition with them as they asked where dad was. It was not easy since I was hurting feeling I had failed them, but the grace of God through the counsel of Bishop Erick and Rev Vicky saw us through. Healing helped me move from military parenting to being a loving mum who was not always yelling. Thank God for God…

# 9

## Living in God's Purpose

Waking up feeling purposeless is incredibly frustrating. You look around and see your friends and coworkers living passionate, engaged, meaningful lives. They have deep relationships, rewarding jobs and a sense of direction that compels them to hop out of bed each morning with a spring in their step.

You know that God has something good in store for you. You don't believe He intends you to live a life of painful drudgery in which each day is a total drag. After all, the Bible is full of verses about joy. While this certainly doesn't mean that every single day is full of laughter, it does mean that an overall sense of gladness should be in your life.

In **Psalm 63:7**, David said, *"for you have been my help, and in the shadow of your wings I will sing for joy."* We always live in God's purpose. Ours is only to recognize His purpose for our lives. God is God and He works all things, including your life, according to his purposes. Nothing can happen without God ordaining it.

**Psalm 57:2** says, *"I cry out to God Most High, to God who fulfills His purpose for me."* This is the key in understanding God's purpose for your life. God has numbered your days and will fulfill every purpose He has for you.

However, our choices and actions also really matter. In some ways, this is a mystery we can't fully understand, but that doesn't mean it's not true. We can choose to do things that will bring us more joy and give us more sense of purpose. But first, here are 6 signs that you don't have much purpose in your life.

**How do you know you are not living in Gods purpose?**
**Lack joy and excitement.** If you wake up every day filled with apathy or dread or total boredom, you're probably not doing what you were meant to do. God has created you uniquely, has really good things planned for you and one of the fruits of the Spirit is joy **(Galatians 5:22)**. Sure, there will be difficult things you encounter that require patience and persistence, but overall you should have a sense of joy and excitement that fills your days, your work and your relationships.

**You don't feel too much fulfillment in life.** If you go about your days experiencing little fulfillment, you may be wandering from your God-given purpose. Fulfillment comes from doing rewarding, meaningful, purposeful things. From a job that taps into your skills and passions. From a relationship that involves giving and receiving. From hobbies that are full of fulfillment instead of mind-numbing.

**You know the feeling of pointless work.** You go to the office, clock in, do your job, then go home and collapse in front of the television. You work for the weekends and for retirement. All true joy you experience comes from things outside of work. From hobbies or friends or side jobs

**Ecclesiastes 8:15** says, *"And I commend joy, for man has nothing better under the sun but to eat and drink and be joyful, for this will go with him in his toil through the days of his life that God has given him under the sun."* Would you say that this kind of joy characterizes your life and work? If not, you may need to rethink where you're headed.

**You feel stuck.** If you desperately want a change but also feel totally stuck in your life, that's almost certainly a sign that you're not walking according to God's purpose. Those who are stuck want to go in a particular direction but don't know how to get there. So they spin their wheels, feeling endlessly frustrated but unsure of how to make the frustration end.

**You have no direction.** If you don't know God's purpose for your life, you constantly feel a sense of aimlessness. You feel as though you're wandering from one thing to another without any forward progress. Nothing excites you and you don't have any specific goals you're working toward. Unlike the Israelites, who wandered for 40 years yet still had a goal (the Promised Land), you don't even have a goal in front of you.

### Ways to discover God's purpose for your life
Even though you feel like you're wandering without any true purpose, that doesn't mean you're lost. You can regain your sense of purpose and discover what God has for your life.

**Go to God in prayer.** If you feel purposeless, ask God to give you wisdom and direction. **James 1:5** states, *"If any of you lacks wisdom, let him ask God, who gives generously to all without reproach, and it will be given him."*

God wants to give you a purpose. He wants to bestow divine wisdom on you. It's not like God is holding out on you to make you miserable. He desires you to have a joyful, ambitious, purposeful life. Ask God for purpose and expect Him to give it to you.

**Read God's word.** The primary way God speaks to us is through the Bible. This means that one of the first things you should do in your search for God's purpose is to start digging into scripture. Now, you won't find any verses that tell you to become a dance instructor or painter, but you will begin to understand the heart of God.

**Psalm 119:105** says, *"Your word is a lamp to my feet and a light to my path."* God's word brings light to paths that otherwise seem dark. In the Bible you learn how to live wisely in God's world, which is the first step towards finding your purpose.

**Realize your gifts and strengths.** God has given you very specific gifts and strengths. Maybe you're a math whiz or a wise counselor. Maybe you have a mind for electronics or business. Maybe you're great at organizing people and getting things done. God's purpose for you probably involves the things you're already good at.

This is where education can be particularly valuable. Learning something new allows you to discover your gifts and then determine how you would use them. It also connects you with people who want to help you towards finding your purpose. Like I said in the earlier pages, in my case I started attending self development programs. Through the programs I met people who challenged me to become better and work towards my goals.

**Determine your passion.** What is one thing you're particularly passionate about? Really, this can be anything from business, art, economics, alleviating poverty or anything else. If money wasn't an issue, what would you love to do?

Determining your passions often helps you figure out what God has called you to do. It's often said that God works at the intersection of our gifts and our passions. Where do your gifts meet your passions? That may be God's purpose for you.

**Get help.**
**Proverbs 11:14** says, *"Where there is no guidance, a people falls, but in an abundance of counselors there is safety."* In other words, one of the main ways God will help you find your purpose is through others. Your counsellors should be people you trust. Whether this is your pastor, professors, parents or friends, it needs to be people who have your back and want the best for you. You want wise counsellors to help you find God's purpose for you. For me my parents in the faith and pastors, Bishop Erick and Rev Vicky Mwangi helped me find my purpose in God.

**Go for a retreat.** Sometimes it can be incredibly helpful to get away from it all and take some unhurried time to think, pray and journal. You don't have to spend a week in the woods for this to be effective. Even just a day away from the hustle and grind can be hugely rewarding.

During these retreats, allow yourself to simply be still. Ponder, ask God for direction and listen for His voice. This doesn't need to be complicated and doesn't require any elaborate rituals. **Hebrews 11:6** is a reminder that

God always rewards those who seek him. He's not hiding in the dark, trying to keep His will hidden from you. He wants to guide you.

**Trust God.** Trying to discover your life purpose can be a stressful, overwhelming thing. It can seem like such a big, confusing, frustrating subject. You want to move forward, but you're not sure how. You want to find your purpose, but you feel like you're aimlessly wandering. But you can trust God to lead you where He wants you to go. As **Psalm 23:2-3** says, *"He leads me beside still waters. He restores my soul. He leads me in paths of righteousness for his name's sake.".* You may feel confused, but God doesn't dwell in confusion and therefore you are assured of His guidance.

In my case, I knew that God had a purpose for my life. God's purpose in my life was for me to serve Him by helping other women to find themselves and get to know Jesus Christ. To work with women who are always burdened by their circumstances. I realized that my journey had a lot of healing for other women. I came to realize that God's purpose in my life was to give hope to women who are in similar situation and mostly to single mums in order for them to view life in a different perspective.

When a woman goes through transition, and there are children involved, you are in it together. You should consider the children in your healing journey. Whatever God has in your life, it doesn't matter how long it will take, God will accomplish it in His own time. Even if you fall, you can rise again. It is very important when you fall to seek help. However, you can always do that when you realize where you are and what you want in your life.

As an individual you need heed to God's voice. This might take a long time, but God's purpose must come to pass. God is very patient and if we keep running He will wait until we get to say yes to Him.

# My Advice to Women

I believe in marriage. Marriage is a gift from God. Marriage is a blessing and it is a good thing that should give you peace. When married women and men are not happy, it is good for them to seek help. It is good for them to seek their inner voice and realize God's purpose for their lives. I did this and it worked for me. I retraced my steps.

Marriage should not be for conformity purposes. One should not do anything to please people. *"Comfort and convenience are not substitute for love"*. Marriage should help bring the best out of you. God created us to have a fulfilled life. Marriage as a gift from God should glorify Him and produce godly offspring for Him.

I advice women to join a church that will embrace them just the way they are. It worked for me and this is why I am a strong woman today. I tell women that going through a separation or divorce can be very difficult, no matter the reason for it.

It can turn your world upside down and make it hard to get through the day work and stay productive. But there are things that one can do to get through the process and stand strong in the end.

They should recognize that it's ok to have different feelings. It's normal to feel sad, angry, exhausted, frustrated and confused and these feelings can be intense. You also may feel anxious about the future. Accept that reactions like these will lessen over time. Even if the marriage was unhealthy, venturing into the unknown is frightening.

Give yourself a break. Give yourself permission to feel and to function at a less than optimal level for a period of time. You may not be able to be quite as productive on the job or care for others in exactly the way you're accustomed to for a little while. No one is superman or superwoman; take time to heal, regroup and re-energize.

Don't go through this alone. Sharing your feelings with friends and family can help you get through this period. Consider joining a support group where you can talk to others in similar situations. Isolating yourself can raise your stress levels, reduce your concentration, and get in the way of your work, relationships and overall health. Don't be afraid to get outside help like therapy or counselling if you need it.

Take care of yourself emotionally and physically. Be good to yourself and to your body. Take time out to exercise, eat well and relax. Keep to your normal routines as much as possible. Try to avoid making major decisions or changes in life plans. Don't use alcohol, drugs or cigarettes as a way to cope; they only lead to more problems.

Avoid power struggles and arguments with your spouse or former spouse. If a discussion begins to turn into a fight, calmly suggest that you both try talking again later and either walk away or hang up the phone.
Take time to explore your interests. Reconnect with things you enjoy doing apart from your spouse. Have you always wanted to take up painting or play on an intramural softball team? Sign up for a class, invest time in your hobbies, volunteer, and take time to enjoy life and make new friends.

Think positively. This may be easier said than done. Things may not be the same, but finding new activities and friends, and moving forward with reasonable expectations will make this transition easier. Be flexible. If you have children, family traditions will still be important but some of them may need to be adjusted. Help create new family activities.

When children are involved, reassure and listen to them. Make sure your children know that your current season in marriage is not their fault. Listen to and ease their concerns, and be compassionate but direct in your responses. Maintain stability and routines for them. Try to keep your children' daily and weekly routines as familiar and stable as possible.

Offer consistent discipline. Now that your children may share time with both parents separately, make sure to agree in advance on everyday decisions and let your children know they can rely on you. Make and keep realistic promises. And don't overly confide in them about your feelings about the separation or divorce.

Don't involve your children in the conflict. Avoid arguing with or talking negatively about the other parent in front of your children. Don't use them as spies or messengers, or make them take sides.

### Walking with other women in ministry

Being a single mum, I have been able to encourage women to know that they can stand again despite falling in their lives and even in their relationships. Pain pushed me higher and gave me desire to help other women who have undergone the same ordeal.

It is good to know that God can still settle you in your single life. One can desire marriage again and settle in God. For those who have separated, I walk with them to rise again and forgive themselves.

For women who have been battered, I tell them that you can find self worth. To know that God can use a broken vessel as there is always hope for a broken vessel.

*"O house of Israel, Said the LORD.*
*Behold, as the clay is in the potter's hand,*
*So are ye in mine hand,*
*O house of Israel."*
**Jeremiah 18:6**

**God can make your life new again.** He sent His prophet Jeremiah to teach this lesson to Israel. In **Jeremiah 18: 1-2,** *"The word which came to Jeremiah from the LORD, saying, Arise, and go down to the potter's house, and there I will cause thee to hear my words."*

Pottery is one of the oldest arts in the world, and it remains virtually unchanged to this present time. The potter would take a lump of clay and twist it, knead it, and pound it until all of the bubbles and impurities were out of it and it was soft and pliable. Then, he would put the clay on his wheel. The potter would throw the lump of clay right in the middle of that wheel, and the wheel would spin. Then, the potter would caress the clay with his talented fingers and smooth it. And from that unlovely, unlikely lump of clay, there would come out a beautiful vessel.

**God is the Potter, and mankind is the clay:** *"Behold, as the clay is in the potter's hand, so are ye in Mine hand, O house of Israel"* God is the master

Workman, and He makes something beautiful out of each one of us lives. There are two things that form the vessel: the touch of the Father's hand and the turning of the wheel. The wheel represents the circumstances of our daily lives. God sees to it that our lives revolve around certain events, and the whole time God is touching our lives and making them what He wants them to be.

As with clay, there are two things that can keep your life from being what it ought to be: The clay might contain a hidden impurity a flaw beneath the surface. Deep down there are some secret things in our lives that nobody knows. This means that the clay is yet to be ready for the potter who is our God to make a vessel in our lives. Maybe it's stiff. The good thing is that just like the broken vessel, there is hope for women who are single mums. I tell single mums that God can take you right now where you are and make out of your life another vessel. God can mend a broken life if you give Him all the pieces. Just turn it over to Him and say, *"Here it is, Lord."* God has made each one of us beautiful and useful.

I have walked with women until they could forgive their husbands and to find help to reconcile again. To help women to know that in this journey it is okay to accept support from their husbands whether in marriage, separated or divorced. I however believe in amicable separation, especially in cases of physical abuse.

I am not self made as I have been doing all this under the *"Mrembo Women's Ministry"* in New Breed City Chapel under the leadership of Rev. Vicky Mwangi.

# 10

# Waiting Bench

**My Season of waiting.**

At a certain point and time, we are all waiting for something. It might be a spouse or a baby. It might be healing or a home. We all find ourselves in the waiting bench at some point in life. Regardless of what we're waiting for, it's easy to feel discontent when things aren't going as planned and our dreams are delayed especially when questions of *'Why?'* and *'How long?'* remain unanswered. God uses seasons of waiting to teach us patience and make us more like Him. But sanctification is not the only purpose God has in mind. When we wait faithfully with unmet longings, we become powerful.

Good things come to those who wait. Anything worth having in life is worth waiting for. The delay makes you even more appreciative because of how long you may have to wait.

As I wait from the Lord I have learnt that waiting is hard but the season is worth it. This is especially when it's obvious that we lack the ability to control the results. Waiting is worth it. I'm learning that waiting on God is actually very important in our relationship with Him and it plays a key role in our spiritual development. Waiting does not have to create bitterness, anger or loss of hope: it can establish a deeper trust and knowledge of who God is and His love for you. I pray that you would experience him intimately as you wait on Him.

### Here are five things that waiting on God has taught me
#### A. I need to cling to the promises found in God's Word.
When I started believing in God's power, I entered into a season of trusting and waiting for God to provide for me in everything. It wasn't easy and at times I felt frustrated that reaching my goal was outside of my control. I searched the word of God for guidance and stumbled upon scriptures on keeping His promises. This is now the framework for how I view my life and specifically, waiting on God.

> In Psalm 130:5, it says,
> "I wait for the Lord, my soul waits, and in his word I hope"

As you wait on God, your hope needs to be in God's promises and not in circumstances, people, or ourselves. Not even in what you hope will happen. The reality is, God's Word will never change nor fade away. Whatever the Bible says (hopes and promises) will  happen because God cannot be unfaithful to Himself

> *"So is my word that goes out from my mouth: It will not return to me empty, but will accomplish what I desire and achieve the purpose for which I sent it.".* **Isaiah 55:11**

The Bible is true, trustworthy, and dependable for all of life and it will not be altered.

Waiting on God feels scary because we lack knowledge about our future, but with the Bible as our foundation, we can be more certain of who God is in a very uncertain world. That always helps me feel more grounded.

### B. God is with me in my waiting (Exodus 33:14)

Moses faced much discouragement in ministry. You can read about it in **Exodus 32 and 33**. He tried to lead the people through the desert, praying and talking to God on their behalf and saving them multiple times from destruction. He was confused as to who would be with him in the journey of being a leader; in the waiting, Moses felt incredibly alone. Moses needed to wait on the Lord to lead and direct him so that he could lead the children of Israel to the promised land.

God responds to Moses: *"My presence will go with you, and I will give you rest"* **Exodus 33:14**. God reassures Moses that he is not alone in his leadership: God tells Moses that He will go with him. Moreover, God's presence will bring deep rest to Moses who desperately needs it.

In the midst of waiting on God, we too can experience that same rest and peace that comes from God's presence. We are never alone in the waiting, no matter how scary or isolating the unknown future feels.

If you have placed your faith in Jesus as Lord, you have been promised the Holy Spirit who dwells in you at all times. He gives you access to God the Father, refreshment, joy, and peace.

In times of waiting, God is always with you; He promises to never leave you, nor turn His back on you **Hebrews 13:5.**

As God is faithful and cannot deny himself, he can never withdraw His presence from you. That's a promise to take to the bank!

### C. I will look more like Jesus after this waiting

The moment you place your faith in Jesus as Savior and Lord, you enter God's family whereby he has predestined you for development and growth.

> *"For we are God's workmanship, created in Christ Jesus to do good works, which God prepared in advance for us to do."*
> **Ephesians 2:10.**

God begins working in our lives to mature and grow us to become more like Jesus. This development begins when we receive the Holy Spirit at conversion, and Jesus promises that he will complete it.

**Phil.1.6** - being confident of this, that he who began a good work in you will carry it on to completion until the day of Christ Jesus.

> *"Being confident of this, that he who began a good work in you will carry it on to completion until the day of Christ Jesus.".*
> **Philippians 1:6**

Another word for the work that he promises to complete is sanctification (spiritual and character development). It is the work of the Holy Spirit in us to make us more like Jesus, stripping away the old, sinful nature, and purifying us. God longs for us to grow to become more like Christ wouldn't it be awful if we never changed but stayed in the same broken and sinful place as when we first realized our need for the gospel?

I'm realizing that it's the periods of waiting on God that my dependence and trust in God deepens. It's in waiting on God where I experience him in fresh and intimate ways. When I turn to Him and seek His guidance, I hear His voice more clearly.

It's in the periods of waiting that my tangible sanctification takes place! Therefore, I'm learning to be grateful and accept these seasons of waiting, because they are a spiritual investment in my future, a future of me that's more like Christ.

### D. God's plans for my life are better than mine. Romans 8:28

When I experience a period of waiting I am tempted to feel as if God has forgotten about my happiness. Doesn't God want me to be happy? Shouldn't He just give me what I want?

I need to remember the truth of who God is. In his wisdom and compassion, He is dedicated to our sanctification. For God, the highest good and ultimate happiness is for us to become more like him. I am grateful for this! The truth is: God is a good father who longs to give us good gifts. **Matthew 7:11** Often, those good gifts come in a package different than what we may expect. The training program that God designs for each of us to become more like Jesus isn't easy or carefree. Like anything of true value it comes with bumps, challenges, and unfulfilled desires. Just because you may feel disappointed or discouraged with the path God is leading you on, doesn't mean you're on the wrong path.

The Apostle Paul writes in

**Romans 8:28,** *"And we know that for those who love God all things work together for good, for those who are called according to His purpose."*

All things (even painful waiting) can work together for God's good in us. God does not call us to brush off the painful, raw, and emotional aspects of waiting, pretending that to have faith in God we must ignore our heart. No, we are to choose to believe that even in the hardest moments of waiting on God, he can transform it into His good, for his purposes which are always a blessing.

### *E. I can trust God to provide for me each day.*
**In Matthew 6:5-13** Jesus instructs his followers how to pray to God and there is one line in verse 11 that always stood out for me:
*"Give us this day our daily bread".*

Essentially it means that we need to take life day by day, praying to God for him to provide just enough for what we need that day. This also reflects God's daily provision to the Israelites when God would provide for them every day in the wilderness by sending bread from the sky. God doesn't send us bread from the sky these days, but through the presence of his Holy Spirit he sustains us each moment, as we walk with him in total surrender.

Naturally, waiting is not comfortable and easy. I want God to give me my *"life loaf"* of bread, the whole thing, not one tiny slice at a time. I want to know each detail of my life story so that I can know what's coming. In a period of waiting on God, it feels painful to not know how things will turn out.

I think though, if God were to tell me my whole life plan, I would most likely run the other direction out of fear. Instead, Scripture teaches us that we are to ask for and receive just enough for one day at a time. Having to wait and depend on God for an unknown future, in God's grace, is the best thing for me to do.

Waiting on God to provide, act, lead, and direct is normal and part of the Christian life. You have all the resources you need to wait on God well, through his Holy Spirit inside of you. Waiting can bring pain and frustration, but waiting well and trusting God each moment of each day will birth new spiritual fruit and blessing in your life.

*How do you make the waiting season hopeful as a child of God?*
**Identify:** What are you waiting on God for? Write it out.
**Pray:** Ask God to provide all your needs and entrust your circumstances to him.
**Trust:** God is good, He loves you, and will complete his work in your life.
**Wait:** Surrender each moment and ask to be filled with the Holy Spirit's power and ability. He will empower you to wait well for God's glory.
**Celebrate:** When God answers prayer or leads you in your waiting, grab a friend and praise Him together! God is worthy of all praises. If He answers your prayer in a way you didn't expect, surrender your expectations and choose to trust God afresh again.

Today, am hungry enough to wait for the right thing which is God's promise for me. You get what you wait for. Strength is renewed as you wait; wings to soar develop as you wait. Waiting builds our dependency on God.

> *My last encounter was supernatural so I will stay on this waiting bench.*
> *"You can't get it if you know it is coming".*
> **Susan Kibe**

Today, I am not where I was back then. It has been a season of discovering me. To truly know yourself is the most important skill you can ever possess. When you know who you are, you know what you need to do, instead of looking for permission from others to do what you already know you ought to do. It allows you to bypass tons of frustration caused by putting time into the wrong things. Yes, life is supposed to be full of trial and error, but this lets you find the best areas for you to experiment with in the first place. Once you know yourself, you will become more confident, you will understand your purpose, and you will begin making a bigger impact on the world.

Steps you need to take in order to know your true self:

### 1. Be quiet
You cannot and will not be able to know yourself until you take the time to be still. Many people don't know themselves because any sort of silence scares them; it's too uncomfortable to be alone with every flaw staring back at them. But it isn't until you get alone, evaluate yourself and are completely truthful with yourself that you will actually be able to see every facet of your life the good and the bad. Be quiet and discover your

true self. Quietness brings us to seasons of authenticity, we get to face and deal with self.

*"Observing yourself is the necessary starting point for any real change."*
**2. Realize who you truly are, not who you want to be.**
I know you already have a set idea of who you desperately want to be, but it might not be who you were designed to be; this is why knowing who you really are is so important. When you know who you are, you will finally see where you and your specific gifts fit into the bigger picture.

And although there are many points along your journey to help you discover yourself, the best way to begin is to take a self-evaluation test. Pin point your top areas of strengths, so you can focus on the change you were meant to bring into the world.

### 3. Find what you are good at
This might be the most difficult step in the process of finding who you are, but it's a necessary one. Sure, it takes trial and error to find what you're good at, and no, I don't want you to give up before you've had more than enough attempts, but knowing when to quit is a gift that everyone needs to learn.

Quit when you've put in ample time and your efforts aren't giving back in return. What is ample time? Only you can decide that. But when you quit correctly, it isn't giving up, it's making room for something better. When your actions do nothing but drain you rather than produce more passion and increase your drive to do more, that's a good sign it is time to focus elsewhere. Your strengths will show you who you are.

#### 4. Find what you are passionate about

Following passion of any kind is a good thing, and you need to pay attention when it comes because it indicates an area of life that you need to pay more attention to. If we're talking about following your passion at work, it's a good thing. And if we're talking about having more passion for life, it's a good thing. Focus more on passion; understand yourself in better ways, and you'll make a bigger impact. Passion produces effort and continuous effort produces results.

#### 5. Ask for feedback

If you don't know yourself, hearing what others have to say about you is a helpful practice. Ask them two simple questions: *"What strengths do you think I need to develop further?"* and *"What weaknesses do you think I need to work on?"* Of course, their opinion isn't going to be perfect, but their feedback will probably indicate a few areas you should at least take a second look at. This step is especially important for those who are stuck in finding themselves. Sometimes those closest to us can see something we might not be able to see in ourselves.

#### 6. Assess your relationships.

A large aspect of knowing yourself can be found in your relationships. When you realize you'll never truly know anyone else until you discover yourself, the importance of knowing yourself becomes even more apparent. This truth especially rings true for business leaders, because if you don't know the people on your team, then you will be lost as a leader. But this rule also applies to any relationship in your life. Almost as much as you need to know yourself, other people also need to know who you are. People need the real you.

Use your reflections to fight your biggest fears, because when you understand who you are meant to be, your purpose will finally become bigger than your fears. When you realize who you are, you will spend less time spinning your wheels. Focusing on your strengths gives you the needed traction to begin making a bigger and better difference in the world. When you know yourself, you will find more peace, and you will find success quicker than ever before. Now go take action and find your true self, starting today.

Today I have a better relationship with my children. I came to realize that I was a bitter mum, a military mum. I was parenting as I was hurting from my past. God has given me joy and healing. I am enjoying parenting my children. I am a happy soul. My relationship with my children has really grown, we can discuss anything about our lives, they ask me questions as they grow. We are able to discuss sexuality and relations that should or should not be without feeling weird.

**Spiritually**

I have grown to a place of knowing that my children look up to me for spiritual guidance and prayers. I take this very seriously and I make declarations on them daily. Teaching them the word of God and how to trust God has helped them grow spiritually. It can only be done by the special grace God.

**Isaiah 54:13 ;-** *All your children shall be taught by the Lord, And great shall be the peace of your children.*

During the Dedication of the newly constructed Temple, Solomon prayed to God, asking Him to forgive and restore the people of Israel when they sinned (**2 Chronicles 6:12-42**). God then told Solomon (in the verse above) that, when the Israelites sinned, they would be restored after going through a four-step process. God's Word is eternal; therefore, this four-step process has unequivocal application to Christians today. Christians are God's people called by His name.

### STEP 1: Humility
The first step in spiritual restoration is humility. To start the restoration process, we must first recognize our nothingness before an Almighty God. I have neither rights nor commendation before God. On my own, I am both guilty and unworthy to be in his Holy presence. God is everything; I am nothing.

### STEP 2: Prayer
The second step in spiritual restoration is prayer. Prayer is an act of humility. Prayer is NOT presenting God with a list of desires. God cares about our needs and He instructs us to *"cast all our cares on Him"* (**1 Peter 5:7**).

> *"Thy kingdom come,*
> *Thy will be done in earth, as it is in heaven."*
> ~**Matthew 6:10**

However, Jesus showed us that the primary purpose of prayer is to prepare persons to perform the perfect will of God (**Matthew 6: 9-13, Luke 22:42**). After we humble ourselves before God, we then seek to discover His will for our lives through prayer.

And He… prayed, saying,
> *"Father, if thou be willing, remove this cup from me: nevertheless, not my will, but thine, be done."*
> **~Luke 22:41-42**

**STEP 3: Communion/Fellowship**
The third step in spiritual restoration is communion with God: 'seeking God's face'. To *'seek God's face'* is to live in His presence: to commune/fellowship with Him. Prayer is the doorway through which we enter into communion with God. Scripture instructs us to seek God, and to do so continually.

To commune/fellowship with God is to live one's life every second as if serving before God's throne in heaven. It is to be in constant dialogue with God. It is to be intimate with God: talking with Him *"face-to-face"*:

> *"Give us this day our daily bread."*
> **~Matthew 6:11**

To *"seek God's face"* is to walk with God as Enoch did: in such close fellowship that the line between earth and heaven becomes blurred. When Moses communed with God he came so close that after the experience his face shone (**Exodus 34:34-35**). God wants to lead us from humility into pr

**STEP 4: Repentance**

The fourth and final step in spiritual restoration is repentance: turning from *"wicked ways"*. Repentance is the offspring of communion. This is not the same *"repentance"* that is a prerequisite for salvation (**Acts 3:19**), because this passage was addressed to *"my people, which are called by my name"*. So, God was addressing those who are already in the fold. Repentance for believers is described in **Romans 12:2** as transformation by a renewing of our minds.

> *"And be not conformed to this world: but be transformed by the renewing of your mind that you may know what good and acceptable perfect will of God is."*
> **Romans 12:2**

God intends to bring us from humility into prayer, from prayer into communion with God and finally communion gives birth to repentance (mental renewal): a change in mindset allows us to turn from our *"wicked ways"*.

These four steps of spiritual restoration, though sequential, are not independent of each other. The believer that humbles himself before The Almighty God will pray, because he recognizes that he must submit to the will of the Lord of Hosts. The believer that discerns the will of God through prayer must also *'seek God's face'*, because to walk in the will of God is to walk in communion with God. And the believer that walks in communion with God cannot help but have his mind renewed.

I am more close to God than I was. I am walking in faith. I have seen God establishing me. My children are growing tremendously. God has restored the years that I lost. I have experienced the faithfulness of God in ways that I cannot explain.

God has showed me that restoration is possible even for someone like me. It is not about the material things but as long as you have Him He is able to give you the desires of your heart.

*"If you find God, You find Gold"*
**Bishop Erick Mwangi**

### Physically
I have been restored physically. I had a successful public life but a very poor private life. God has reversed that. Today I am a happy soul, the joy of the Lord is indeed my strength. I am at peace with myself and my surroundings. God has given me beauty for ashes, He literally changed my garments.

### Navigating through the season
I am navigating through this season learning the word of God every day. I have been learning the word of God that is appropriate for this season.

I do not do anything that the Lord has not directed me to do. This has preserved me so far. In God's master plan everyone is created with many things in common.

I came to realize that God has a great plan, a vision. And that vision includes you. Yes, it does, or you would not be here. You are special. You are different from anyone else. The great Creator, God personally designed and made you that way. Therefore, you have a contribution to offer that no one else can make.

It is said that the difference between a chump and a champ is dedication, and dedication demands purpose, faith and vision-daily vision.

Having vision means being able to visualize. Visualizing is the beginning of fulfilled vision. When we think of an apple, we see it in our mind's eye.

Christians have vision and are able to dream the impossible dream. A man or woman of vision (of faith) fully believes the impossible dream is possible. I believe in this type of vision. How about you?

**God's master plan**
In God's master plan everyone is created with many things in common with everyone else. Yet each person is distinct from any other human being.

In God's sight you are not a washout. You are not a complete failure. You are not a hopeless sinner. God says you are worth having. You are worth loving. God's greatest physical creation is you.

Accept this fact: You have value and are not inferior to anyone. We are all wonderfully different and unique. Remember, you are God's idea; and He never makes a mistake. You were not made to be exactly like any other person. But each of us was made for a purpose. God had a vision about you and has a vision for you. If you don't know God's present and ultimate

**vision for you personally, right now, let me share it with you.**

*"And it shall come to pass in the last days, says God, that I will pour out of My Spirit on all flesh; your sons and your daughters shall prophesy, your young men shall see visions, your old men shall dream dreams"* **Acts 2:17.**

The apostle Paul summarizes God's will and vision for all humanity in a nutshell:

*"... God our Savior desires all men to be saved and to come to the knowledge of the truth"*
**1 Timothy, 2:3-4.**

God, through His Son Jesus Christ, reveals the knowledge of truth Paul is referring to: *"For God so loved the world that He gave His only begotten Son, that whoever believes in Him should not perish but have everlasting life. For God did not send His Son into the world to condemn the world, but that the world through Him might be saved"* **John 3:16-17**

That is God's vision prepared and outlined for mankind, including you. It is the offering of, and the way to, eternal life in the kingdom of God: *"That whoever believes in Him should not perish but have eternal life"* **John 3:15.** *"They will come from the east and the west, from the north and the south, and sit down in the kingdom of God"* **Luke 13:29.**

But is such a thing really possible? Maybe you are skeptical. Well, so were some of Jesus' disciples.

*"But Jesus looked at them and said, `With men it is impossible, but not with God; for with God all things are possible"* **Mark 10:27.**

There's the answer. Jesus said all things are possible to him who really believes they are possible, and according to God's will.

> In **Acts 2:38-39,** *the apostle Peter outlines the process, the steps, to begin fulfilling God's vision for you. "Then Peter said to them, `Repent, and let every one of you be baptized in the name of Jesus Christ for the remission of sins; and you shall receive the gift of the Holy Spirit. For the promise is to you and to your children, and to all who are afar off, as many as the Lord our God will call."*

Christ then begins to live within you through the indwelling of the Holy Spirit **Colossians 1:27; Ephesians 3:16-17.**

In the book of Romans, God continues to explain His personal vision for you, *"But if the Spirit of Him who raised Jesus from the dead dwells in you, He who raised Christ from the dead will also give life to your mortal bodies through His Spirit who dwells in you"* **Romans 8:11.**

In subsequent verses He nails down in detail His ultimate purpose and vision for you: your magnificent destiny, why you were born. *"For if you live according to the flesh you will die; but if by the Spirit you put to death the deeds of the body, you will live. For as many as are led by the Spirit of God, these are sons of God"* **Romans 8:13-14.**

Hard to believe, but true. Your destiny envisioned by the Creator God is to become His very own son or daughter. His child, His family, His heirs. Read on in **Romans 8:16-17:** *"The Spirit Himself bears witness with our spirit that we are children of God, and if children, then heirs-heirs of God and joint heirs with Christ ..."* There is not, nor can there be, a greater hope or destiny.

**Will you act to fulfill God's vision for you?** Those called now are invited to be living examples of a better way, a richer and fuller life. You are called to the joy of sharing God's vision for mankind with others, called to be trendsetters in high moral values and conduct, in physical and spiritual integrity. You are called to leadership through service, called to son ship. *"But as many as received Him, to them He gave the right to become children of God, to those who believe in His name"* **John 1:12.**

The Head of the Church, Jesus Christ, does change lives, and for the better. Christians, bought and paid for by the death and blood of Christ, have been wonderfully invited by God to join Him in His vision for mankind. In baptism, we covenant with Him and fully dedicate our lives to His purpose for us.

In **Matthew 20:26-28** Jesus said, *"...But whoever desires to become great among you, let him be your servant. And whoever desires to be first among you, let him be your slave-just as the Son of Man did not come to be served, but to serve, and to give His life a ransom for many."*

While still in this life, your opportunity is *"by the mercies of God, that you present your bodies a living sacrifice, holy, acceptable to God, which is your reasonable service"* **(Romans 12:1).** Wherever you are, work every day to be the best person you can be, doing the best you can do with what you have to do with, to the glory of God. Yes, this is your destiny, God's vision for you.

Ladies should not get into relationships leading into marriage seeking to be complete. You are already a complete person the way you are. We realize that when we do anything to be complete we make mistakes. Today I have sober judgment on everything that I do

## Lessons Learnt From my Life

As I journeyed through my life through the seasons, I confirmed that healing is possible. Every story is different and the healing is also personal. Nobody can ride on the journey of another person. This is because loss of relationships affects us differently. Healing becomes personal by first accepting what happened, dealing with what was your fault and letting go of what is beyond you. Most times we delay healing by carrying burdens that are beyond us. Anything in life that you have no control over should not be a hindrance to taking the necessary steps towards progress.

Healing also comes when we forgive ourselves for the mistakes we made, bad decisions we took, and allow the grace of God to work in us. Most times even as believers we pray for forgiveness and do not set ourselves to receive forgiveness. Receiving forgiveness sets us free from guilt and the baggage of our pain. Only then can we be able to heal from the pain and move on with life.

Healing also means you release the other person, in this case your spouse. Failing to release the hurt makes one to be like a debt collector. Harboring un-forgiveness is said to be like taking poison and expecting the other person to die. It does not matter what happened but as Christians we are called to forgive by the grace of God. It is not an easy stage of healing and it does not happen immediately, but once it does happen it is the most liberating part of the journey.

Personally it took me lots of prayer and counsel from my pastors Bishop Erick and Rev Vicky Mwangi. Affirmation from my parents and siblings too kept me going. One thing I will forever be grateful to God for is the love I have received from my family throughout all seasons of my life. I had to keep reminding myself that I was still loved by God regardless, that the mistake hadn't taken me from the love of God. **Romans 8:38-39**

One of the major therapies besides counseling and prayer is hiding in the word of God. Being vulnerable before God always gives us a safe landing. This is the time to keep speaking the word of God over the situation. **Ephesians chapter1** was a very reassuring scripture to remind me that I am chosen, I am redeemed, I am adopted by God, marked for inheritance in Jesus Christ. That was enough affirmation to keep me going.

The word of God also encourages us to walk with each other. I was assigned a task to walk with other women going through loss of relationships, separation or divorce under the Women's Ministry called Mrembo at New Breed City Chapel. Pouring myself into these women, holding heir hands and praying with them made me stronger. God used my healing to encourage them, because they could see someone who had been through a similar journey and gotten over it.

Healing brings back the joy that helps us to laugh again. I am a testimony that after all the tears and pain you can still laugh again. It has to be a deliberate effort to find back your joy in God. The bible tells us that the joy of the Lord is our strength; **Nehemiah 8:10** and that with joy we shall draw from the wells of salvation, **Isaiah 12:3** That means that for a believer your joy is not debatable, because it's a fruit of the holy spirit.

Most of the mental health cases arising from loss of relationships are as a result of lacking joy, failing to forgive ourselves, and blaming ourselves about issues beyond our control. We need the help of God to dwell in joy because it is His desire. By the grace of God one can really laugh again.

Another lesson that comes with healing is that restoration is very possible. Most people out of pain lock themselves out of restoration but it is indeed possible to love again and continue living. The bible is very clear in **Joel 2:25** that God will restore what we lost. For those who desire marriage, God is able to bring about healing and reconciliation. For those who were not married like me but had desired to the point of getting entangled, God is able to bring the desires to pass according to his will.

# 11

## My Garment of Praise

*He hath made every thing beautiful in his time*
    **{Ecclesiastes 3:11}.**
*This is my Story in a nut shell. A life that God has beautified.*

By the grace of God, I am at a beautiful place. Went through the valley of the shadow of death and I pulled through to the other side. I sailed through many waters and they didn't overwhelm me. God leveled mountains for me. He made what looked like crooked paths, straight. He has given me songs of Victory.

I have gone through healing, taken my children through healing, forgiven myself of the past and released every baggage from my past relationships. I have been made whole.

God restored me and gave me purpose in his house. I was and still am totally sold out to the work of the ministry. While serving in New breed chapel, I met this great Gentleman in church by the name Frank Atsulu. we were not even friends, I had seen his face so many times as he was in charge of the sound in church and I was a girl in love with the Lord and serving there as a pastor.

Along the journey Frank lost his wife and was left to raise his 5 children by himself. That was a big blow for him and as a church we stood by him and God graciously carried him through that hard season. Two years after the loss he approached me, with intentions of taking me out. That got me off guard. Him of all the people! Without giving it a second thought, I declined his request. I was very concerned about his healing and did not want to commit myself to a man who was in pain.

After two months of him being consistent in the request, I gave him a chance to hear him out.

Frank meant serious business. He wanted a wife out of me, shoes that looked too big for me to fit in. So I also asked him to allow me to pray about it, which was the right thing for me to do.

So much was involved if I said yes. First this gentleman had another wife who went to be with the Lord. That meant the man may still be in grief. Secondly He had five children who lost a mother. How do I step in and be their mother? third I had two of my own children, how will they accept this man as their father?. How will all these children blend and bond together to make a family?.

All this was going through my mind and in that state God led me to shalom. A place of ultimate peace about the whole issue. God started ministering to me that I may realize that my pain was to mould me for the assignment ahead. The bible says He makes all things beautiful and Yes He was making everything beautiful for me behind the scenes.

God took away my fears concerning the children I was going to take in. God connected my children with Frank in a remarkable way. The two elder daughters of Frank whom I feared might resent me, God miraculously intertwined us so well.

The Bible says that God's ways are higher than our own ways, these same girls I was worried about received me as their mum in the most amazing manner. The boys were easy and they also embraced us very well. The family blended by the grace of God.

That day came when I had to introduce Frank to my family. That was the most overwhelming day ever. It marked the dawning of a new day for us.

I thought God had restored me but my own mother had been restored twice. Prayers she had made many years back and she constantly prayed were being answered right in her eyes. She had always desired to have more grandchildren, older ones too. That answer came through my settling in marriage. The reception Frank received in our home compound was beyond words.

It was like a lost son coming back home. Frank connected with my dad so well and my parents blessed us and months after that I walked down the aisle and said Yes I do to the most amazing man I've ever met.

I stepped into a marriage that was purposeful. God wiped away our different tears and He clothed us with a garment of gladness.

Two families came together and we became one big beautiful family To the Glory of God.

I thank God that anytime we are together as a family the joy is a testimony of God's plan for us.

Marriage has brought so much fulfillment to me, my biological children too were excited to have a present daddy in their lives. My daughter Hadassah used to pray everyday, the joy of being in this family is evident everytime you see her smile. I never dreamt that I would have a large family, not to mention seven children, but it has brought my parenting to another level as I wear 7 hats as a mum. It's such a beautiful blessing.

**Indeed God is a restorer.**
When I look at my life, the seasons moulded me into the person I am today. The lessons were not wasted, the pain birthed a ministry and a well of wisdom that can give some guidance on people getting into relationships.

Well, I wouldn't say I have achieved it all, I am still on my journey into fulfilling purpose by the grace of God. What I would say is that I have ticked one prayer point that has been a constant on my journal and moved onto a different matter. One thing am really grateful for in this season is the counsel I received to get me where I am. The prayers my parents have prayed for me have been answered as they see.

It feels good to see the manifestation of God's word over my life. I give God all the glory for preservation into this season. I also appreciate the season of waiting because I now see what the preparation was about.

It is at the threshing floor where pressing is done. As pressing is done and refining takes place only one thing can be produced, the anointing.

I clearly understand the purpose of my marriage as to offer hope to other women. Those who feel like the waiting has been long, those who have been hurt and didn't understand the purpose of the pain. I believe that God takes us through our journeys even to encourage others. Today I can confidently tell another lady that God answers even that prayer point that seems to have taken long, we just need to find purpose.

## My Heart Beat

*I want to be an institution that brings transformation to a woman.*
I want to reach out to a woman who feels like she lost herself through sexual assault as a young girl. It is my desire to have the message out that we can arise and shine, shed the victim mentality and impact lives as victors. Our scars of the past should shine so brightly to offer healing to new cases upcoming every other day.

Sister girl, it was not your fault, it wasn't even about your dressing or where you found yourself at that particular time. The perpetrator was the sick one, and ours is to release them to God their creator.

My desire is for you the reader, to know that there is life beyond that past and the pain that you may have encountered. Looking at life beyond the pain requires great faith and hope in God, that is why this book has been written as a source of hope. I believe that we should face our scars from the past as seeds that our generations will benefit from.

*I want to provide rescue centers for women going through abuse.* To be able to pour myself into girls who are finding their identity and women who may have lost their identity. I want to help a woman balance who she really is and who the world thinks she is. I want to help a woman unmask and face any situation that hinders her from becoming who God intended her to be. This can only happen through authenticity that is made possible by creating a safe space.

*My healing journey came through several safe places;* New Breed Chapel's Women Ministry- Mrembo, Noble Womanhood Program by Faith Muriithi, Transform Nations (Ezer and Intentional Mum programs).

Authenticity means that one is able to express who they are without fear of judgement. Anytime an opportunity arises to share one's journey without fear of being judged, healing will happen. Creating the atmosphere for authenticity is one thing that should be worked at, at all cost.

I desire that this book can be a guide to you my reader, in your pursuit of purpose. By the scriptures from the word of God, the journey of my life and the counsel I have received, it is my prayer that you find direction. The seasons of our lives are meant to yield resourceful content that can help other people. That is why I have been as authentic as possible to help you see that God can restore, heal and indeed give beauty for ashes.

*I am a testimony that there is no ash too much for God to beautify.* I am also a testimony that God comes when we wait upon Him. He rewards the wait when it is upon Him. He renews our strength as we wait upon Him. I believe that if the pain I went through was for the world to be a better place for another woman, it was worth it.

I refuse to waste my tears and the seasons I went through in the making of my testimony.

I believe that it must count for something by the grace of God.

# 12

# Epilogue

I have shared out my life and my pursuit in being gracefully broken and made whole again. I have made myself most vulnerable to allow you the reader to copy and paste shamelessly what you think works for you while you may cut and discard what does not work for you.

Healing comes through the help of the holy spirit and authenticity. I have written this book in a state of vulnerability to enable the reader to connect with my life. We all have very diverse stories and circumstances, how we go through into victory is what unites us. Going through loss of a relationship, sexual abuse, struggling to find your identity and purpose could not be your case, but the solution is Jesus Christ.

I am a living testament that there is no mess God cannot clean up and turn into a message. There is no pain that He cannot turn into power for his glory. God is a restorer, and He doesn't just restore what you lost, He goes exceedingly beyond our thoughts and expectations. God's grace comes as the fourth man in the fire to make us not even smell of smoke from our journeys.

I have seen God lift me from the miry clay literally, He has made me not to look like the pain I went through. He can do the same for you dear reader, even so much more because He is not a respecter of persons. The journey you have come through this far could have been bumpy. We serve a living God who levels mountains, makes every crooked path straight and that situation is not an isolated case. Surrender to Him and let His power carry you as I have done. You will testify as He turns that situation around.

The Chinese have a saying that *"A journey of one thousand miles begins with a single step"*. I appeal to you to make that single step to allow God to mold you as He desires. Your life does not need to be summarized by that situation. You can rise again, dust every dirt and walk with your head held high to claim your crown. It is not over until God draws the curtains of your life.

***Keep moving.***

www.ingramcontent.com/pod-product-compliance
Lightning Source LLC
Chambersburg PA
CBHW061659120626
46550CB00003B/1005